ALL ABOUT WORDS: SPECTACULAR SENTENCES

ALL ABOUT WORDS: SPECTACULAR SENTENCES

SUSAN WINEBRENNER et al

ReadersMagnet, LLC

All About Words: Spectacular Sentences
Copyright © 2023 by Susan Winebrenner et. al.

Published in the United States of America
ISBN   Paperback: 978-1-960629-31-9
ISBN   eBook: 978-1-960629-32-6

All rights reserved. No part of this publication may be reproduced, stored in a retrieval system or transmitted in any way by any means, electronic, mechanical, photocopy, recording or otherwise without the prior permission of the author except as provided by USA copyright law.

The opinions expressed by the author are not necessarily those of ReadersMagnet, LLC.

ReadersMagnet, LLC
10620 Treena Street, Suite 230 | San Diego, California, 92131 USA
1.619. 354. 2643 | www.readersmagnet.com

Book design copyright © 2023 by ReadersMagnet, LLC. All rights reserved.

Cover design by Ericka Obando
Interior design by Dorothy Lee

TABLE OF CONTENTS

Dedications	7
Susan's Note To Educators	9
Avoid Pygmalion in the Classroom	9
Focus on Student Autonomy in Sentence Selection	10
Your Word List	10
Your Student's Spectacular Sentences	10
Teachers: Directions For Use	12
It's Ok To Peek	12
Before You Start	12
For Those in a Physical Classroom	13
For Those in a Virtual Classroom	13
For Either Type Of Classroom	14
Getting Students Started on Using Spectacular Sentences	14
Rubric For Small Group Work	16
Spectacular Sentences: Part One	17
Nine Parts of Speech (POS):	18
How to Identify the Correct Part of Speech	19
Analyzing Basic Sentences	19
Constructing More Complex Sentences	20
Pronunciation Key	21
Spectacular Sentences: Part Two	22
Spectacular Sentences: Answer Key	92
Record Keeping Forms	160
Your Own Word List	163

DEDICATIONS

Susan Winebrenner dedicates this book to her loyal friend, **Tito Jude Callueng,** for his willingness to create the necessary time for this work so it could be included in this book. Without him, it would not have happened.

Stephanie Rosson-Niess dedicates her work on this book to her beautiful mom, **Peggy Ann Rosson,** who has had a profound influence on her life by always encouraging her to reach for the stars, and to her remarkable daughter **Amanda,** who is an exceptional writer poised to create her own books soon.

Carolyn Stillman dedicates her work to her supportive husband **Jim** and lovely family who really appreciate her – always have and always will! Maybe that's because she is so supportive and lovely herself.

All the authors dedicate this book to **Patricia Perez,** a long-time educator and friend of Susan's who was drafted into editing service while she thought she was simply visiting Susan. Her editing work was done with good humor and amazing time dedication. Thank you, Pat. We might still be in a draft stage without your miraculous assistance!

We also send thanks to Susan's sometimes co-author, **Lisa Kiss** and her husband **Doug** for making an emergency visit to Susan to help with the final editing process.

Finally, the writers would like to thank Susan's amazing and extremely helpful daughter, **Kari B. Naimon** for her attention to detail on this book and her moral support to help get her part done.

SUSAN'S NOTE TO EDUCATORS

To the educators using this book in their classrooms, welcome to the new, revised version of what was formerly titled Super Sentences. We are so happy to have you here!

As Louie, a 6th grade student I taught once said, "Guess what, Mrs. Winebrenner! You know how I study editorial cartoons wherever I can find them? Well, they just started using lots of the same words you are using in these vocabulary-building sentences!"

YES, LOUIE, WE APPRECIATE YOUR OBSERVATION!

I know you will also observe the excitement and enthusiasm in the kids (and even adults) with whom you share these sentences. Just get started…and watch it happen.

Avoid Pygmalion in the Classroom

Research by Robert Rosenthal and others starting in the 1950s **_(The Pygmalion Effect)_** demonstrates how we educators communicate our unspoken expectations about a student's learning capacity in what can sometimes be harmful ways. It is quite shocking! This research demonstrates that what matters more than what we tell them is how accountable we make them feel with what they are learning in many more ways than written tests! When a teacher makes specific choices about the level **they believe** kids can handle, they inadvertently tell them VOLUMES about their general expectations regarding whether they think that kid can succeed or not.

To help deter the unintended Pygmalion Effect, we ask that the kids (rather than you, the teacher) choose several sentences from which each group will be able choose the one they want to translate. This gives students a sense of ownership in the work that they do, making the work itself more fun – and even more importantly, the learning is more likely to stick.

Focus on Student Autonomy in Sentence Selection

Many of your students might decide to either not work on a particular sentence or choose only the easier ones. In this revised edition, the sentences are arranged from easier to more difficult instead of according to grade level or age. Students should self-select their sentences which ultimately encourages and increases intrinsic motivation. As they are successful with easier sentences, they will become more comfortable with attempting more challenging ones.

Your Word List

To keep the fun going even when your students are not working on the sentences, show them how to use the 'YOUR WORD LIST' table at the end of this book which provides a space for them to keep track of words they don't know the meaning of at their first encounter. Students should enter **one word at a time in the 'word' column (not the part of speech or meaning)** before continuing with their work. At a time designated by you, students should work to complete the center and right columns of their charts for words they have not already been able to define.

Your Student's Spectacular Sentences

Whenever a student creates THEIR OWN Spectacular Sentence that really impresses you, **please show them how to post it to my website**. www.susanwinebrenner.com. Click on "submit your spectacular sentences here" (note that in order to post the sentence on our site for others to benefit from, we will need consent from a parent or guardian provided by completing the entry form on the next page and emailing it to me at skwine76@gmail.com. It would be especially helpful if 'Spectacular Sentence' is in the subject line).

SPECTACULAR SENTENCES ENTRY FORM

I hereby grant permission for Susan Winebrenner and/or her affiliates to use the submitted Spectacular Sentence on her website and/or in other materials they create and/or distribute.

_____   _____   _____
Name (Please Print)   Age   Current Grade in School

_____
City/State/Province/Country

_____
Signature of Parent or Guardian

To check to see if your student's sentence has been posted, please visit my website (www.susanwinebrenner.com) and go to the section on SPECTACULAR SENTENCES.

We really hope you and your students enjoy this book!

All the very best in your spectacular sentence journey!

Susan Winebrenner, February 2024

TEACHERS: DIRECTIONS FOR USE

This book contains thirty-four SPECTACULAR SENTENCES at a variety of difficulty levels as well as one bonus sentence. In addition, we have included an example of how to use each sentence in everyday language. However, your student's sentences do not need to exactly mirror those translations. Their sentences need only reflect a similar meaning.

As students work through this book, they will:

- learn how to use the dictionary, thesaurus, and pronunciation keys
- learn to comprehend the syntax and parts of speech of the words in their sentence
- apply skills learned in reading, English, and language arts
- analyze the most sensible way to put words together for coherent meaning
- evaluate how well the sentences create meaningful thoughts, and
- become enthusiastic about their own lifetime vocabulary development.
- You may wish to purchase extra copies of this book so that all students/participants can write in the book or if you decide to duplicate and use the paper copy that is also fine.

It's OK To Peek

Note that all the answers to the sentences can be found in the Answer Section later in this book (in case both the student and you get stuck). Because the answers are contained in this same book, some of you might worry that students will "peek" at them before trying the work themselves. This is actually ok because as they check answers, students will gain enough confidence with the sentences and then feel comfortable challenging themselves to "try first and check later" (I still do this with acrostic puzzles that have challenged me for decades. When I start solving a puzzle, I use only pencil and check all the answers I have attempted in the answer key before I move on to the next step of entering those letters into the quotation part of the puzzle. "Cheating??" Not really. Am I making sure I don't create mistake upon mistake… and completely mess up the puzzle? Yes – for sure! Besides, while all these things are happening, I am repeating words and definitions in my mind many times over, always learning along the way.)

Before You Start

Since these activities are so challenging, we suggest that students work together in pairs or triads so they may constantly check out the sense of their work with each other.

For the best learning outcomes, we also suggest that the groups of students choose their own sentences from the entire list available as the teacher reads them aloud to the whole class and listeners write down the sentence numbers of their selected sentences until all groups have chosen three sentences.

It's perfectly fine if more than one group chooses the same sentence.

Prior to starting work on the chosen sentences, each student should have a copy of the sentences their group selected as well as an unabridged dictionary. Make sure the chosen dictionary talked in the language of your students so it shouldn't be so difficult that they will be bamboozled by the level of difficulty. Some teachers buy thesaurus to keep with their dictionary because it seems to be equally useful.

Make sure you have a range of grade-level dictionaries and/or thesauri available. Keep in mind that your advanced students will likely need dictionaries or thesauri that are written for higher grade levels. Likewise, readers who are struggling with the content may need a dictionary or thesaurus that is less advanced than their current grade level.

For Those Using this Material in a Physical Classroom:

We recommend making it easy for learners to not lose their chosen sentences by having each student write their names on their sentence papers first. Then, have each group select a sentence monitor who controls the flow of papers in and out of their group's sentence collection. However, only the sentence monitor should remove or add sentence papers to their group's collection.

For Those Using this Material in a Virtual Classroom:

Have the students decide individually whether they want to print the worksheets and work on paper or work on their sheets online. Create a dropbox or other file sharing space where all completed sheets can be stored and accessed later. Similar to those in a physical classroom, each group should select a sentence monitor who will control the flow of documents in and out of their file sharing space. We suggest that only that person should remove or add sentence documents to their group's collection.

ALL ABOUT WORDS: SPECTACULAR SENTENCES

For Those Using this Material for either Type of Classroom:

When it's time to work on the sentences, the selected monitor should distribute one copy of their chosen sentence to each student so they can take turns reading the sentences aloud several times to their groupmates. Then, have students work together in pairs or triads to:

- analyze the most sensible way to put the words together to create a coherent meaning
- talk about whether they are seeing words they want to add to their "MY WORDLIST" (located toward the end of this book)
- talk about where they have noticed some of these words in other settings.

Have groups continue working on the same sentence and use their dictionary to identify the parts of speech illustrated by each capitalized word. At this point, have the students share this information with others in their group.

For each word, ask students to use the best abbreviation for the part of speech that relates to the target word. We recommend you teach only two parts of speech per lesson, then slowly add other parts of speech while reviewing those already learned.

If there are disagreements, encourage the students to use their dictionaries to resolve them. We recommend pairing nouns, pronouns, and adjectives, verbs with adverbs, and other parts in ways that make sense to you and your students. Also remember to review previously mastered parts of speech concepts each time you teach a new lesson.

Getting Students Started on Using Spectacular Sentences

1. Choose one sentence from the first half of the sentences in the book and use either as a whole group lesson to model the tasks or as a small group activity to set the stage for future independent self-selected work.
2. Distribute one copy of the chosen sentence so students can take turns reading the sentence aloud several times to unpack the sentence and discover contextual clues that might help them identify the meaning and part of speech of each capitalized and bolded word. As you unpack these sentences, you will likely discover many opportunities to practice some of the standard(s) you are addressing in your instruction.
3. Regardless of whether the students work on these individually or with partners, they should use the chart included with every sentence. If there

are students who prefer to create their own completed products (i.e., collaborative posters, multi-media representations) instead of completing a chart, let them go! We have found the ownership of the learning is intrinsically motivating.

4. Students who work with partners to complete the task can take turns reading the sentence, selecting a different word for everyone to work on and then sharing with their group.
5. If you wish to add an additional element, students with the same word can work collaboratively with others in class and then go back to their original group to share their information. If teachers notice students entering information that does not align with the context of the sentence, have them return to their expert group and rediscuss their findings. Well-worded questions might help them "discover" new insights to the meaning of the word.
6. Once groups have completed their sentences, encourage them to create and rehearse a presentation of their words to the entire class. If there are reluctant students, arrange a special guest, another teacher, a principal, or any staff member the students know and have them present it to them in a small group.

If grading is required **(which is not recommended because it may restrict creativity)**, each member of the small group should get the same grade. The grade should reflect the effort in completing the sentence task.

For grading purposes, students could work together to create a rubric (a sample generic rubric is included below) that could then be used for evaluation. A word of caution however — testing students on the words out of context (i.e., vocabulary list tests) will not give the teacher a true picture of students' understanding of the word meaning and appropriate use. Additionally, these type of memorization tests will likely extinguish their enthusiasm for the activity.

Rubric for Small Group Work

Use this form with small groups of students to help them learn how to work more effectively together. Review each component one at a time, starting with the one that needs the most attention, then working through them to eventually include all the behaviors.

_____ _____
Student Name   Date of Observation

What working in a group looks like	Excellent (4)	Very Good (3)	Good (2)	Needs Practice (1)	TOTAL
Helps others to participate					
Stays on task					
Follows group rules					
Shares ideas					
Total					

SPECTACULAR SENTENCES PART ONE

NINE PARTS OF SPEECH (POS):

The following pages can be used as a resource for your students. Distribute as you see fit.

1. **Nouns** are a person, place, thing, or idea. They can take on a variety of roles in a sentence. They are capitalized when they're the official name of something or someone, called proper nouns in these cases. Examples: pirate, Caribbean, ship, freedom, Captain Jack Sparrow.

2. **Pronouns** "stand in" for nouns in a sentence. They are more general versions of nouns that refer to people, places, or things. Examples: I, you, he, she, it, ours, them, who, which, anybody, ourselves.

3. **Verbs** are words that tell the action(s) nouns are doing in a sentence. They can also show a feeling of a noun, such as "Most children love candy." Verbs change form based on the time in which the action is happening, such as: "I buy. She bought it. They will buy it." These differences are called verb tenses (present, past, future). Examples: sing, dance, believes, seemed, finish, eat, drink, be.

4. **Adjectives** give more information about nouns and pronouns. They specify which one, how much, what kind, and more. Adjectives allow readers and listeners to use their senses to imagine something more clearly. Examples: hot, lazy, funny, unique, bright, beautiful, poor, smooth.

5. **Adverbs** describe verbs, adjectives, and even other adverbs. Many adverbs end in -ly. They specify when, where, how, and why something happened and to what extent or how often. Examples: softly, lazily, often, only, hopefully, softly, sometimes.

6. **Prepositions** tell the relationship between a noun or pronoun and the other words in a sentence. They may be found at the start of a phrase which contains a preposition and its object (called a prepositional phrase). Examples: up the road, over the bridge, against the wall, by the fire, for my grandkids, into the pool, close to each other, or apart from my family.

7. **Conjunctions** join words, phrases, and clauses in a sentence. Examples: and, but, or, so, yet, with.

8. **Articles and Determiners** are the "a, an, the" words that precede nouns to provide a flow in the sentence. Other determiners: These crayons are beautiful. Those hotdogs were huge.

9. **Interjections** are expressions that can stand on their own or be contained within sentences. These words and phrases often show strong emotions and are followed by an exclamation mark (!). Examples: ah, whoops, ouch, yabba dabba do!

HOW TO IDENTIFY THE CORRECT PARTS OF SPEECH

Only interjections (**Hooray!**) have a habit of standing alone. Every other part of speech must be contained within a sentence. Other parts of speech come in many varieties and may appear just about anywhere in a sentence.

To know for sure what part of speech a word falls into, look not only at the word itself but also at its meaning, position, and use in a sentence.

For example, in the first sentence below, '**work**' functions as a noun; in the second sentence, a verb.

*Lapita showed up for **work** two hours late.*

- The noun **'work'** is the thing Lapita shows up for.

He will have to work until midnight.

- The verb **'work'** is the action he must perform.

Learning the names and uses of the basic parts of speech is just one way to understand how sentences are constructed.

Analyzing Basic Sentences

To form a basic complete sentence, you only need two elements: a noun (or pronoun standing in for a noun) and a verb.

Quiz yourself or a partner about the questions below.

- Is *Birds fly.* a complete sentence?
- Why or why not?
    - In the short sentence above, 'birds' is the noun and 'fly' is the verb. The sentence makes sense and gets the point across.

You can have a sentence with just one word without breaking any sentence formation rules. The short sentence below is complete because it's a command to an understood "you".

- *Go!*

Here, the pronoun "you", standing in for a noun, is **understood** to be there and acts as the subject. The sentence is really saying, "(You) go!"

Constructing More Complex Sentences

Use more parts of speech to add additional information about what's happening in a sentence to make it more complex. Take the first sentence from above, for example, and incorporate more information about how and why birds fly.

- Birds fly when migrating before winter.
- 'Birds' and 'fly' remain the noun and the verb, but now there is more description of when birds fly.

PRONUNCIATION KEY

Note: Teachers and parents have the author's permission to make copies of this document as needed.

ə	as in banana, level	sh	as in shout, shy
a	as in pad, fat	th	as in thread, thick
ā	as in made, vacation	th	as in this, neither
ä	as in all, saw	u	as in fun, hum
ch	as in check	ü	as in school, rule
e	as in bed, met	u̇	as in foot, put
ē	as in meat, free	âr	as in far
i	as in did, lip	ār	as in air, dare
ī	as in died, mine	êr	as in perk
j	as in juice, just, gentle	ēr	as in ear, weird
k	as in cookie, kitchen	îr	as in sir
ng	as in finger, sing	ôr	as in fort
o	as in hot, pod	ûr	as in fur
ō	as in home, know	yu	as in youth, few
oi	as in destroy, boy, noise	u̇r	as in cure, fury
oy	as in boy, joy	zh	as in vision
oo	as in ooze, boo	kw	as in quail
ow	as in pout, fowl		

To add or change sounds in the pronunciation key, go to www.ipa.com (international phonics association).

SPECTACULAR SENTENCES PART TWO

SPECTACULAR SENTENCE #1

An **ABSENT-MINDED** professor, whose summer **HABITAT** was a **DISMAL SHANTY**, was **FLABBERGASTED** to learn he had been **DULY BEQUEATHED** a **FASHIONABLE, PALATIAL MANSION** in a **LUXURIOUS, GENTEEL** neighborhood.

WORD	PART OF SPEECH ABBREVIATION	PRONUNCIATION	MEANING (IN SIMPLE LANGUAGE)
absent-minded			
habitat			
dismal			
shanty			
flabbergasted			
duly			
bequeathed			
fashionable			

ALL ABOUT WORDS: SPECTACULAR SENTENCES

WORD	PART OF SPEECH ABBREVIATION	PRONUNCIATION	MEANING (IN SIMPLE LANGUAGE)
palatial			
mansion			
luxurious			
genteel			

© Winebrenner, S. Rosson-Niess, S. & Stillman, C. (2024) Spectacular Sentences. San Diego: readersmagnet.com

Translation into Everyday Language

_____
_____
_____
_____
_____

Student's Name: _____

Classroom Name or Number: _____

SPECTACULAR SENTENCE #2

We live near a **GROTESQUE, HIDEOUS, DETERIORATED** old house, filled with **TORTUOUS, IMPENETRABLE** hallways which give me **EERIE, GHASTLY** feelings of **CLAUSTROPHOBIA** and **TREPIDATION**, especially when I hear the **FORMIDABLE CACOPHONY** of **BABBLING** voices when no one is there!

WORD	PART OF SPEECH ABBREVIATION	PRONUNCIATION	MEANING (IN SIMPLE LANGUAGE)
grotesque			
hideous			
deteriorated			
tortuous			
impenetrable			
eerie			
ghastly			

ALL ABOUT WORDS: SPECTACULAR SENTENCES

WORD	PART OF SPEECH ABBREVIATION	PRONUNCIATION	MEANING (IN SIMPLE LANGUAGE)
claustrophobia			
trepidation			
formidable			
cacophony			
babbling			

© Winebrenner, S. Rosson-Niess, S. & Stillman, C. (2024) Spectacular Sentences. San Diego: readersmagnet.com

Translation into Everyday Language
_____
_____
_____
_____
_____

Student's Name: _____
Classroom Name or Number: _____

SPECTACULAR SENTENCE #3

A ten-year-old boy was a dedicated **BIBLIOPHILE** and his twelve-year-old sister was an extraordinary **VERBIVORE**. They laughed so hard when they started tickling each other, they fell **CATTYWAMPUS** onto the floor where a **KERFUFFLE** began until their mom came to investigate. The children instantly fell into **CAHOOTS** and even increased their **EXTRAORDINARY VERBIGERATIONS** until their mom became even more **BUMFUZZLED** and **EXCORIATED** them more angrily than she intended.

WORD	PART OF SPEECH ABBREVIATION	PRONUNCIATION	MEANING (IN SIMPLE LANGUAGE)
bibliophile			
verbivore			
cattywampus			
kerfuffle			
in cahoots			
extraordinary			
verbigerations			

ALL ABOUT WORDS: SPECTACULAR SENTENCES

WORD	PART OF SPEECH ABBREVIATION	PRONUNCIATION	MEANING (IN SIMPLE LANGUAGE)
bumfuzzled			
excoriated			

© Winebrenner, S. Rosson-Niess, S. & Stillman, C. (2024) Spectacular Sentences. San Diego: readersmagnet.com

Translation into Everyday Language

_____
_____
_____
_____
_____

Student's Name: _____

Classroom Name or Number: _____

SPECTACULAR SENTENCE #4

My uncle, an **OBESE GOURMAND,** with his usual **APLOMB,** approached the table at my cousin's wedding **BANQUET** with such **ALACRITY** (**OBVIOUSLY** lacking **ADEQUATE FORESIGHT**) that he **INGESTED** what he thought was a **PALATABLE DELICACY,** which was actually the table's centerpiece. How **GAUCHE**!

WORD	PART OF SPEECH ABBREVIATION	PRONUNCIATION	MEANING (IN SIMPLE LANGUAGE)
obese			
gourmand			
aplomb			
banquet			
alacrity			
obviously			
adequate			

ALL ABOUT WORDS: SPECTACULAR SENTENCES

WORD	PART OF SPEECH ABBREVIATION	PRONUNCIATION	MEANING (IN SIMPLE LANGUAGE)
foresight			
ingested			
palatable			
delicacy			
gauche			

© Winebrenner, S. Rosson-Niess, S. & Stillman, C. (2024) Spectacular Sentences. San Diego: readersmagnet.com

Translation into Everyday Language

_____
_____
_____
_____
_____

Student's Name: _____

Classroom Name or Number: _____

SPECTACULAR SENTENCE #5

The speaker showed his **ACUITY** on the subject while most of the students' faces bore a **STULTIFIED** expression, even though the speaker **PRESSED ON** with his **BRINKMANSHIP** that pushed the listeners to **UBIQUITOUSLY EXCORIATE** his techniques with their shared **PALPABLE** displeasure. This created an **ARDUOUS** continuation of the **RECALCITRANT** speaker's attempts to persuade the listeners that if they accepted his **TRANCENDENTAL** truths and blindly continued to accept his **OBFUSCATIONS** of accurate facts, they would eventually understand his message.

WORD	PART OF SPEECH ABBREVIATION	PRONUNCIATION	MEANING (IN SIMPLE LANGUAGE)
acuity			
stultified			
pressed (on)			
brinkmanship			
ubiquitously			
excoriate			
palpable			

ALL ABOUT WORDS: SPECTACULAR SENTENCES

WORD	PART OF SPEECH ABBREVIATION	PRONUNCIATION	MEANING (IN SIMPLE LANGUAGE)
arduous			
recalcitrant			
transcendental			
obfuscations			

© Winebrenner, S. Rosson-Niess, S. & Stillman, C. (2024) Spectacular Sentences. San Diego: readersmagnet.com

Translation into Everyday Language

_____
_____
_____
_____
_____

Student's Name: _____

Classroom Name or Number: _____

SPECTACULAR SENTENCE #6

I faced the **CATACLYSMIC** event with what I hoped was an **ENIGMATIC** expression, hiding my usual **EGREGIOUS NATURE** and **NEFARIOUS** thoughts, proceeding with **TREPIDATION** and **DREAD** to shout my **APPEALS** into the surrounding **QUAGMIRE**, hoping I would soon find some **CAMARADERIE**.

WORD	PART OF SPEECH ABBREVIATION	PRONUNCIATION	MEANING (IN SIMPLE LANGUAGE)
cataclysmic			
enigmatic			
egregious			
nature			
nefarious			
trepidation			
dread			

ALL ABOUT WORDS: SPECTACULAR SENTENCES

WORD	PART OF SPEECH ABBREVIATION	PRONUNCIATION	MEANING (IN SIMPLE LANGUAGE)
appeals			
quagmire			
camaraderie			

© Winebrenner, S. Rosson-Niess, S. & Stillman, C. (2024) Spectacular Sentences. San Diego: readersmagnet.com

Translation into Everyday Language

_____
_____
_____
_____
_____

Student's Name: _____
Classroom Name or Number: _____

SPECTACULAR SENTENCE #7

My parents **AGONIZED** over whether to buy me a computer game with which I was **ENAMORED**, or a radio-controlled airplane, which I **LOATHED**. My **BERSERK** behavior let them know I was **DEVASTATED** by their choice, and they let me know they **RESENTED** my **OBJECTIONABLE, REBELLIOUS, TEMPERAMENTAL** reaction, and **ADMONISHED** me **EARNESTLY** to remember that everyone is **FALLIBLE**.

WORD	PART OF SPEECH ABBREVIATION	PRONUNCIATION	MEANING (IN SIMPLE LANGUAGE)
agonized			
enamored			
loathed			
berserk			
devastated			
resented			
objectionable			

ALL ABOUT WORDS: SPECTACULAR SENTENCES

WORD	PART OF SPEECH ABBREVIATION	PRONUNCIATION	MEANING (IN SIMPLE LANGUAGE)
rebellious			
temperamental			
admonished			
earnestly			
fallible			

© Winebrenner, S. Rosson-Niess, S. & Stillman, C. (2024) Spectacular Sentences. San Diego: readersmagnet.com

Translation into Everyday Language
_____
_____
_____
_____

Student's Name: _____
Classroom Name or Number: _____

SPECTACULAR SENTENCE #8

For a career in **AERONAUTICS**, **PREREQUISITES** include: a **DAUNTLESS**, **HEROIC** spirit, no **QUEASINESS** or **ACROPHOBIA**, the ability to **SKILLFULLY** operate **TECHNICAL APPARATUS**, and an **ENERGETIC DEVOTION** to the **GLORY** of American **DOMINANCE** in space.

WORD	PART OF SPEECH ABBREVIATION	PRONUNCIATION	MEANING (IN SIMPLE LANGUAGE)
aeronautics			
prerequisites			
dauntless			
heroic			
queasiness			
acrophobia			
skillfully			
technical			

ALL ABOUT WORDS: SPECTACULAR SENTENCES

WORD	PART OF SPEECH ABBREVIATION	PRONUNCIATION	MEANING (IN SIMPLE LANGUAGE)
apparatus			
energetic			
devotion			
glory			
dominance			

© Winebrenner, S. Rosson-Niess, S. & Stillman, C. (2024) Spectacular Sentences. San Diego: readersmagnet.com

Translation into Everyday Language

_____
_____
_____
_____
_____

Student's Name: _____

Classroom Name or Number: _____

SPECTACULAR SENTENCE #9

The **AUDACITY** of his actions, despite the **PAUCITY** of available logical outcomes, led to the **AMBIVALENCE** of **PROPOUNDED** solutions which reflected the **PROSAIC** nature of his followers to discover a cure for the **MIASMA** of the swamp in question. The group created an **APHORISM** to describe this **MATTER AT HAND**: "Birds of a feather usually flock together", **ENCAPSULATING** the **PLETHORA** of poor ideas being explored by the group. As a reader, you are **AT LIBERTY** to create your own **APHORISM** describing this situation and send it to Susan at skwine76@gmail.com.

WORD	PART OF SPEECH ABBREVIATION	PRONUNCIATION	MEANING (IN SIMPLE LANGUAGE)
audacity			
paucity			
ambivalence			
propounded			
suggested			
prosaic			
miasma			

ALL ABOUT WORDS: SPECTACULAR SENTENCES

WORD	PART OF SPEECH ABBREVIATION	PRONUNCIATION	MEANING (IN SIMPLE LANGUAGE)
aphorism			
matter-at-hand			
encapsulating			
plethora			
at liberty			

© Winebrenner, S. Rosson-Niess, S. & Stillman, C. (2024) Spectacular Sentences. San Diego: readersmagnet.com

Translation into Everyday Language

_____
_____
_____
_____
_____

Student's Name: _____

Classroom Name or Number: _____

SPECTACULAR SENTENCE #10

Listening to the **LOQUACIOUS** gentleman's tale of his **AVARICIOUS** behavior in his **AUDACIOUS** pursuit of fame and wealth, I was struck by his **VORACIOUS** nature and his **DISINGENUOUS** ability to appear **VIVACIOUS** and even **OBSEQUIOUS** even though his actions were clearly **DUPLICITOUS** and **TREACHEROUS**.

WORD	PART OF SPEECH ABBREVIATION	PRONUNCIATION	MEANING (IN SIMPLE LANGUAGE)
loquacious			
avaricious			
audacious			
voracious			
disingenuous			
vivacious			
obsequious			

WORD	PART OF SPEECH ABBREVIATION	PRONUNCIATION	MEANING (IN SIMPLE LANGUAGE)
duplicitous			
treacherous			

Add any words ending in '-ous' that you encounter from other reading sources.

WORD	PART OF SPEECH ABBREVIATION	PRONUNCIATION	MEANING (IN SIMPLE LANGUAGE)

© Winebrenner, S. Rosson-Niess, S. & Stillman, C. (2024) Spectacular Sentences. San Diego: readersmagnet.com

Translation into Everyday Language

_____
_____
_____
_____
_____

Student's Name: _____

Classroom Name or Number: _____

SPECTACULAR SENTENCE #11

The **HEBETUDINOUS, LETHARGIC SCHOLAR** moved very slowly as though he was **DISTRACTED** from his learning, which he claimed to love for its own sake. He also claimed he was suffering from **CLINOMANIA** and his **THRASONICAL** behaviors caused his classmates to accuse him of trying to disturb their own learning with his **MALARKEY**. When his classmates discovered that he was also **ABIBLIOPHOBIC**, they wondered if he would ever be **SHREWD** enough to demonstrate his self-claimed **SAGACITY**.

WORD	PART OF SPEECH ABBREVIATION	PRONUNCIATION	MEANING (IN SIMPLE LANGUAGE)
hebetudinous			
lethargic			
scholar			
distracted			
clinomania			
thrasonical			
malarkey			

ALL ABOUT WORDS: SPECTACULAR SENTENCES

WORD	PART OF SPEECH ABBREVIATION	PRONUNCIATION	MEANING (IN SIMPLE LANGUAGE)
abibliophobic			
shrewd			
sagracity			

© Winebrenner, S. Rosson-Niess, S. & Stillman, C. (2024) Spectacular Sentences. San Diego: readersmagnet.com

Translation into Everyday Language

_____
_____
_____
_____
_____

Student's Name: _____
Classroom Name or Number: _____

SPECTACULAR SENTENCE #12

The **BRAGGADOCIO** of the **POETASTER** is apparent as he writes his **CLOYING DITHYRAMBS** for **ACCOLADES** alone; while the **ORGULOUS IAMBOGRAPHER** has the **METTLE** and **PANACHE** to **EXCOGITATE** his **LAMPOONS** without **GASCONADE**.

WORD	PART OF SPEECH ABBREVIATION	PRONUNCIATION	MEANING (IN SIMPLE LANGUAGE)
braggadocio			
poetaster			
cloying			
dithyrambs			
accolades			
orgulous			
iambographer			
mettle			

ALL ABOUT WORDS: SPECTACULAR SENTENCES

WORD	PART OF SPEECH ABBREVIATION	PRONUNCIATION	MEANING (IN SIMPLE LANGUAGE)
panache			
excogitate			
lampoons			
gasconade			

© Winebrenner, S. Rosson-Niess, S. & Stillman, C. (2024) Spectacular Sentences. San Diego: readersmagnet.com

Translation into Everyday Language

_____
_____
_____
_____
_____

Student's Name: _____

Classroom Name or Number: _____

SPECTACULAR SENTENCE #13

In **CARTOMANCY**, **PRESTIDIGITATORS** who use **OBFUSCATION** and **PETTIFOGGERY** may live in **OBLOQUY** if a **CHARY**, **INDEFECTIBLE HARBINGER** of justice arises whose **ONUS** is to expose the **FEIGNED VERISIMILITUDE** of the practitioners as **CHICANERY**.

WORD	PART OF SPEECH ABBREVIATION	PRONUNCIATION	MEANING (IN SIMPLE LANGUAGE)
cartomancy			
prestidigitators			
obfuscation			
pettifoggery			
obloquy			
chary			
indefectible			
harbinger			

ALL ABOUT WORDS: SPECTACULAR SENTENCES

WORD	PART OF SPEECH ABBREVIATION	PRONUNCIATION	MEANING (IN SIMPLE LANGUAGE)
onus			
feigned			
verisimilitude			
chicanery			

© Winebrenner, S. Rosson-Niess, S. & Stillman, C. (2024) Spectacular Sentences. San Diego: readersmagnet.com

Translation into Everyday Language

_____
_____
_____
_____
_____

Student's Name: _____

Classroom Name or Number: _____

SPECTACULAR SENTENCE #14

The **CAITIFF USURPER**, **ACCOUTERED** for **MARAUDING** with his **JUNTA**, sought **IMPERIUM** for the **MOBOCRACY,** unaware of the **ANIMUS** of the **IMPUISSANT, LUMPEN DEMURRERS** ready to **IMMOLATE** themselves for the sake of their cause.

WORD	PART OF SPEECH ABBREVIATION	PRONUNCIATION	MEANING (IN SIMPLE LANGUAGE)
caitiff			
usurper			
accoutered			
marauding			
junta			
imperium			
mobocracy			
animus			

ALL ABOUT WORDS: SPECTACULAR SENTENCES

WORD	PART OF SPEECH ABBREVIATION	PRONUNCIATION	MEANING (IN SIMPLE LANGUAGE)
impuissant			
lumpen			
demurrers			
immolate			

© Winebrenner, S. Rosson-Niess, S. & Stillman, C. (2024) Spectacular Sentences. San Diego: readersmagnet.com

Translation into Everyday Language

_____
_____
_____
_____
_____

Student's Name: _____
Classroom Name or Number: _____

SPECTACULAR SENTENCE #15

Because she had **DETECTED CHRONIC DEFICIENCIES** in our spelling recently, our teacher declared an **ULTIMATUM**: either we **RECTIFY** the **DECLINE** in our scores and **ACCRUE** several **CONSECUTIVE TRIUMPHS**, or we would have to **FORFEIT** our place as the **FOREMOST CONTRIBUTORS** to the school newspaper.

WORD	PART OF SPEECH ABBREVIATION	PRONUNCIATION	MEANING (IN SIMPLE LANGUAGE)
detected			
chronic			
deficiencies			
ultimatum			
rectify			
decline			
accrue			

ALL ABOUT WORDS: SPECTACULAR SENTENCES

WORD	PART OF SPEECH ABBREVIATION	PRONUNCIATION	MEANING (IN SIMPLE LANGUAGE)
consecutive			
triumphs			
forfeit			
foremost			
contributors			

© Winebrenner, S. Rosson-Niess, S. & Stillman, C. (2024) Spectacular Sentences. San Diego: readersmagnet.com

Translation into Everyday Language

_____
_____
_____
_____

Student's Name: _____
Classroom Name or Number: _____

SPECTACULAR SENTENCE #16

In the **FABULOUS, GRANDIOSE CHATEAU**, which has an **INCOMPARABLY IMPRESSIVE, PANORAMIC** view of the surrounding **TERRAIN**, the **GORGEOUS CHANDELIER** swayed **OMINOUSLY**, seconds before the **LETHAL** earthquake struck.

WORD	PART OF SPEECH ABBREVIATION	PRONUNCIATION	MEANING (IN SIMPLE LANGUAGE)
fabulous			
grandiose			
chateau			
incomparably			
impressive			
panoramic			
terrain			
gorgeous			

ALL ABOUT WORDS: SPECTACULAR SENTENCES

WORD	PART OF SPEECH ABBREVIATION	PRONUNCIATION	MEANING (IN SIMPLE LANGUAGE)
chandelier			
ominously			
lethal			

© Winebrenner, S. Rosson-Niess, S. & Stillman, C. (2024) Spectacular Sentences. San Diego: readersmagnet.com

Translation into Everyday Language

_____
_____
_____
_____
_____

Student's Name: _____

Classroom Name or Number: _____

SPECTACULAR SENTENCE #17

At the **FESTIVE, TESTIMONIAL REPAST** for our **FLAMBOYANT, DAPPER, DEBONAIR** principal, the guests ate **RAVENOUSLY** all the **DELECTABLE TIDBITS** which had been **PAINSTAKINGLY** prepared by our P.T.A.'s **ENTERPRISING** experts in the **CULINARY** arts.

WORD	PART OF SPEECH ABBREVIATION	PRONUNCIATION	MEANING (IN SIMPLE LANGUAGE)
festive			
testimonial			
repast			
flamboyant			
dapper			
debonair			
ravenously			
delectable			

ALL ABOUT WORDS: SPECTACULAR SENTENCES

WORD	PART OF SPEECH ABBREVIATION	PRONUNCIATION	MEANING (IN SIMPLE LANGUAGE)
tidbits			
painstakingly			
enterprising			
culinary			

© Winebrenner, S. Rosson-Niess, S. & Stillman, C. (2024) Spectacular Sentences. San Diego: readersmagnet.com

Translation into Everyday Language

_____
_____
_____
_____
_____

Student's Name: _____

Classroom Name or Number: _____

SPECTACULAR SENTENCE #18

The **FETCHING** young woman with the **INTRIGUING** ability to **MESMERIZE** those around her was sometimes able to experience **UPWARD MOBILITY** which filled her heart with **EUPHORIA** and her bank account with **WINDFALLS**. These abilities appear to protect her from **BELLICOSE ENCOUNTERS** and **SPASMS** of internal fear about her future.

WORD	PART OF SPEECH ABBREVIATION	PRONUNCIATION	MEANING (IN SIMPLE LANGUAGE)
fetching			
intriguing			
mesmerize			
upward mobility			
euphoria			
windfalls			
bellicose			

ALL ABOUT WORDS: SPECTACULAR SENTENCES

WORD	PART OF SPEECH ABBREVIATION	PRONUNCIATION	MEANING (IN SIMPLE LANGUAGE)
encounters			
spasms			

© Winebrenner, S. Rosson-Niess, S. & Stillman, C. (2024) Spectacular Sentences. San Diego: readersmagnet.com

Translation into Everyday Language

_____
_____
_____
_____
_____

Student's Name: _____

Classroom Name or Number: _____

SPECTACULAR SENTENCE #19

At the circus, a **FOOLHARDY, LOQUACIOUS HAWKER** stood in a **GARGANTUAN, GARISHLY** decorated wagon, trying to **BAMBOOZLE** and **BEFUDDLE** the people in the crowd, using **LINGO** to sell them a **CONCOCTION** which he **ASSERTED** would allow kids to **PROCURE** all 'A's in school if they **IMBIBED** one teaspoonful every morning.

WORD	PART OF SPEECH ABBREVIATION	PRONUNCIATION	MEANING (IN SIMPLE LANGUAGE)
foolhardy			
loquacious			
hawker			
gargantuan			
garishly			
bamboozle			
befuddle			

ALL ABOUT WORDS: SPECTACULAR SENTENCES

WORD	PART OF SPEECH ABBREVIATION	PRONUNCIATION	MEANING (IN SIMPLE LANGUAGE)
lingo			
concoction			
asserted			
procured			
imbibed			

© Winebrenner, S. Rosson-Niess, S. & Stillman, C. (2024) Spectacular Sentences. San Diego: readersmagnet.com

Translation into Everyday Language
_____
_____
_____
_____
_____

Student's Name: _____

Classroom Name or Number: _____

SPECTACULAR SENTENCE #20

The **MEWLING, INCONTINENT NEONATES** are **PURPORTED** to **REEK VENIAL, NOISOME FETORS** similar to those **EMANATING** from a **NOXIOUS, MEPHITIC CARAVANSERAI**.

WORD	PART OF SPEECH ABBREVIATION	PRONUNCIATION	MEANING (IN SIMPLE LANGUAGE)
mewling			
incontinent			
neonates			
purported			
reek			
venial			
noisome			
fetors			

ALL ABOUT WORDS: SPECTACULAR SENTENCES

WORD	PART OF SPEECH ABBREVIATION	PRONUNCIATION	MEANING (IN SIMPLE LANGUAGE)
emanating			
noxious			
mephitic			
caravanserai			

© Winebrenner, S. Rosson-Niess, S. & Stillman, C. (2024) Spectacular Sentences. San Diego: readersmagnet.com

Translation into Everyday Language

_____
_____
_____
_____
_____

Student's Name: _____

Classroom Name or Number: _____

SPECTACULAR SENTENCE #21

She appeared to be having trouble with several **IMPEDIMENTS** so that her sermon was full of **EQUIVOCATION** and thus was received with **MERETRICIOUS PERSIFLAGE** and **PROFLIGATE** disbelief even though she had a **PANACHE** about her. Unfortunately, several of the communicants viewed that attitude as **MENDACIOUS** and thus labeled her an **INVETERATE** liar.

WORD	PART OF SPEECH ABBREVIATION	PRONUNCIATION	MEANING (IN SIMPLE LANGUAGE)
impediments			
equivocation			
meretricious			
persiflage			
profligate			
panache			
mendacious			

ALL ABOUT WORDS: SPECTACULAR SENTENCES

WORD	PART OF SPEECH ABBREVIATION	PRONUNCIATION	MEANING (IN SIMPLE LANGUAGE)
inveterate			

© Winebrenner, S. Rosson-Niess, S. & Stillman, C. (2024) Spectacular Sentences. San Diego: readersmagnet.com

Translation into Everyday Language
_____
_____
_____
_____
_____

Student's Name: _____
Classroom Name or Number: _____

SPECTACULAR SENTENCE #22

"Automan", the **MECHANICAL, AMBIDEXTROUS** robot we own to do our **MENIAL** chores, caused a **FRENETIC HULLABALOO** when his **CIRCUITS** became **INOPERABLE**, and he ran **AMOK CAPRICIOUSLY** through our house, **DEFACING** everything in his path and leaving **IMPASSABLE PANDEMONIUM** everywhere.

WORD	PART OF SPEECH ABBREVIATION	PRONUNCIATION	MEANING (IN SIMPLE LANGUAGE)
mechanical			
ambidextrous			
menial			
frenetic			
hullabaloo			
circuits			
inoperable			

ALL ABOUT WORDS: SPECTACULAR SENTENCES

WORD	PART OF SPEECH ABBREVIATION	PRONUNCIATION	MEANING (IN SIMPLE LANGUAGE)
amok			
capriciously			
defacing			
impassable			
pandemonium			

© Winebrenner, S. Rosson-Niess, S. & Stillman, C. (2024) Spectacular Sentences. San Diego: readersmagnet.com

Translation into Everyday Language

_____
_____
_____
_____
_____

Student's Name: _____

Classroom Name or Number: _____

SPECTACULAR SENTENCE #23

The **MEED** for the **PROFLIGATE GORMANDIZER**, whose **IRREFRAGABLY CORPULENT PHYSIOGNOMY** betrayed his refusal to hold in **ABEYANCE** his **DRACONIC** appetite, was **DYSPEPSIA** and **KATZENJAMMER**.

WORD	PART OF SPEECH ABBREVIATION	PRONUNCIATION	MEANING (IN SIMPLE LANGUAGE)
meed			
profligate			
gormandizer			
irrefragably			
corpulent			
physiognomy			
abeyance			
draconic			

ALL ABOUT WORDS: SPECTACULAR SENTENCES

WORD	PART OF SPEECH ABBREVIATION	PRONUNCIATION	MEANING (IN SIMPLE LANGUAGE)
dyspepsia			
katzenjammer			

© Winebrenner, S. Rosson-Niess, S. & Stillman, C. (2024) Spectacular Sentences. San Diego: readersmagnet.com

Translation into Everyday Language
_____
_____
_____
_____
_____

Student's Name: _____

Classroom Name or Number: _____

SPECTACULAR SENTENCE #24

The visiting **PRELATE, INDAGATING MULTIFARIOUS** aspects of **TRADITIONALISM** by virtue of his **ACUMEN**, labored in the **CHANCEL** by the **SACRISTY** door, resisting the impulse to **SQUIB** a **POLEMICAL PAEAN** which would have been a **CONTRETEMPS** to his colleagues in the **CALEFACTORY**.

WORD	PART OF SPEECH ABBREVIATION	PRONUNCIATION	MEANING (IN SIMPLE LANGUAGE)
prelate			
indagating			
multifarious			
traditionalism			
acumen			
chancel			
sacristy			

ALL ABOUT WORDS: SPECTACULAR SENTENCES

WORD	PART OF SPEECH ABBREVIATION	PRONUNCIATION	MEANING (IN SIMPLE LANGUAGE)
squib			
polemical			
paean			
contretemps			
calefactory			

© Winebrenner, S. Rosson-Niess, S. & Stillman, C. (2024) Spectacular Sentences. San Diego: readersmagnet.com

Translation into Everyday Language

_____
_____
_____
_____
_____

Student's Name: _____

Classroom Name or Number: _____

SPECTACULAR SENTENCE #25

A **PLUVIOPHILE** finds **EUPHORIA** when the weather is **FORBIDDING** as it often **SUPPRESSES** an urge to **ENGAGE IN KLEPTOMANIA**. If one is in a place where **COLLOQUIALISMS** are the norms, they might seem to protect the **DISGRUNTLED** from **BELLICOSE** activity and **PAROXYSMS** of **OVERWHELMING** fear.

WORD	PART OF SPEECH ABBREVIATION	PRONUNCIATION	MEANING (IN SIMPLE LANGUAGE)
pluviophile			
euphoria			
forbidding			
suppresses			
engage (in)			
kleptomania			
colloquialisms			

ALL ABOUT WORDS: SPECTACULAR SENTENCES

WORD	PART OF SPEECH ABBREVIATION	PRONUNCIATION	MEANING (IN SIMPLE LANGUAGE)
disgruntled			
bellicose			
Paroxysm(s)			
overwhelming			

© Winebrenner, S. Rosson-Niess, S. & Stillman, C. (2024) Spectacular Sentences. San Diego: readersmagnet.com

Translation into Everyday Language

_____
_____
_____
_____
_____

Student's Name: _____

Classroom Name or Number: _____

SPECTACULAR SENTENCE #26

The **PRODIGIOUS** and **PROLIFIC COGNOSCENTE** of modern music, **FESTINATING** to **TRANSCRIBE** the **SCHERZO** for winds and **TIMPANI**, **TRUNCATED** it to make a **SEGUE** between the **ITERATIVE, ANTIPHONAL**, and **ISACOUSTIC** sections of his new composition.

WORD	PART OF SPEECH ABBREVIATION	PRONUNCIATION	MEANING (IN SIMPLE LANGUAGE)
prodigious			
prolific			
cognoscente			
festinating			
transcribe			
scherzo			
timpani			

ALL ABOUT WORDS: SPECTACULAR SENTENCES

WORD	PART OF SPEECH ABBREVIATION	PRONUNCIATION	MEANING (IN SIMPLE LANGUAGE)
truncated			
segue			
iterative			
antiphonal			
isacoustic			

© Winebrenner, S. Rosson-Niess, S. & Stillman, C. (2024) Spectacular Sentences. San Diego: readersmagnet.com

Translation into Everyday Language

_____
_____
_____
_____
_____

Student's Name: _____

Classroom Name or Number: _____

SPECTACULAR SENTENCE #27

The **TRUCULENT, OPPIDAN LICKSPITTLE SEQUESTERED** himself from the **BROUHAHA** caused by the **PUSILLANIMOUS MOUNTEBANK** and **MACHINATED** a **MACHIAVELLIAN PREVARICATION** to **METE** to himself some of the mountebank's **LUCRE**.

WORD	PART OF SPEECH ABBREVIATION	PRONUNCIATION	MEANING (IN SIMPLE LANGUAGE)
truculent			
oppidan			
lickspittle			
sequestered			
brouhaha			
pusillanimous			
mountebank			
machinated			

ALL ABOUT WORDS: SPECTACULAR SENTENCES

WORD	PART OF SPEECH ABBREVIATION	PRONUNCIATION	MEANING (IN SIMPLE LANGUAGE)
Machiavellian			
prevarication			
mete			
lucre			

© Winebrenner, S. Rosson-Niess, S. & Stillman, C. (2024) Spectacular Sentences. San Diego: readersmagnet.com

Translation into Everyday Language
_____
_____
_____
_____
_____

Student's Name: _____
Classroom Name or Number: _____

SPECTACULAR SENTENCE #28

Tigers can be **SAVAGE, FEROCIOUS, COMBATIVE** animals. Tiger trainers should not be too **ARROGANT** or **CONCEITED**, or they might have to **GRAPPLE DEFENSIVELY** with a **VORACIOUS, BELLIGERENT CARNIVORE** that would **APPARENTLY** be **VICTORIOUS**.

WORD	PART OF SPEECH ABBREVIATION	PRONUNCIATION	MEANING (IN SIMPLE LANGUAGE)
savage			
ferocious			
combative			
arrogant			
conceited			
grapple			
defensively			
voracious			

ALL ABOUT WORDS: SPECTACULAR SENTENCES

WORD	PART OF SPEECH ABBREVIATION	PRONUNCIATION	MEANING (IN SIMPLE LANGUAGE)
belligerent			
carnivore			
apparently			
victorious			

© Winebrenner, S. Rosson-Niess, S. & Stillman, C. (2024) Spectacular Sentences. San Diego: readersmagnet.com

Translation into Everyday Language

_____
_____
_____
_____
_____

Student's Name: _____

Classroom Name or Number: _____

SPECTACULAR SENTENCE #29

The **SENESCENT MYSTAGOGUE**, **DIVAGATING** from **LUCULENT** interpretations and **SPOUTING ABSTRUSE CANT, MESMERIZED** the **PURBLIND NEOPHYTES** who were **AGOG** at his supposed **SAGACITY**.

WORD	PART OF SPEECH ABBREVIATION	PRONUNCIATION	MEANING (IN SIMPLE LANGUAGE)
senescent			
mystagogue			
divagating			
luculent			
spouting			
abstruse			
cant			
mesmerized			

ALL ABOUT WORDS: SPECTACULAR SENTENCES

WORD	PART OF SPEECH ABBREVIATION	PRONUNCIATION	MEANING (IN SIMPLE LANGUAGE)
purblind			
neophytes			
agog			
sagacity			

© Winebrenner, S. Rosson-Niess, S. & Stillman, C. (2024) Spectacular Sentences. San Diego: readersmagnet.com

Translation into Everyday Language

_____
_____
_____
_____
_____

Student's Name: _____

Classroom Name or Number: _____

SPECTACULAR SENTENCE #30

The **UNCONSCIONABLE MALFEASANTS** of the **KAKISTOCRACY** had a **PROCLIVITY** to **PRATE INDEFATIGABLY** in their own **ARGOT** and would **JUGULATE** any **TIMOROUS PROSELYTE** who held an opinion **MINACIOUS** or **PARLOUS** to them.

WORD	PART OF SPEECH ABBREVIATION	PRONUNCIATION	MEANING (IN SIMPLE LANGUAGE)
unconscionable			
malfeasants			
kakistocracy			
proclivity			
prate			
indefatigably			
argot			
jugulate			

ALL ABOUT WORDS: SPECTACULAR SENTENCES

WORD	PART OF SPEECH ABBREVIATION	PRONUNCIATION	MEANING (IN SIMPLE LANGUAGE)
timorous			
proselyte			
minacious			
parlous			

© Winebrenner, S. Rosson-Niess, S. & Stillman, C. (2024) Spectacular Sentences. San Diego: readersmagnet.com

Translation into Everyday Language

_____
_____
_____
_____
_____

Student's Name: _____

Classroom Name or Number: _____

SPECTACULAR SENTENCE #31

In my **SOLITUDE**, I find **SERENDIPITY** when other **AFFICIONADOS**, who are **UBIQUITOUS** in my **QUAINT, IDYLLIC** neighborhood, over-populated by **XENOPHOBES** with a **PARLANCE** all their own, sometimes become actually **OBSTREPEROUS** when they discover the **CONUNDRUMS**, they are discussing are the **EPITOME** of senselessness.

WORD	PART OF SPEECH ABBREVIATION	PRONUNCIATION	MEANING (IN SIMPLE LANGUAGE)
solitude			
serendipity			
afficionados			
ubiquitous			
quaint			
idyllic			
xenophobes			

ALL ABOUT WORDS: SPECTACULAR SENTENCES

WORD	PART OF SPEECH ABBREVIATION	PRONUNCIATION	MEANING (IN SIMPLE LANGUAGE)
parlance			
obstreperous			
conundrums			
epitome			

© Winebrenner, S. Rosson-Niess, S. & Stillman, C. (2024) Spectacular Sentences. San Diego: readersmagnet.com

Translation into Everyday Language

_____
_____
_____
_____
_____

Student's Name: _____

Classroom Name or Number: _____

SPECTACULAR SENTENCE #32

On a **CHIVY** with our **FOWLING PIECES**, we approached the **CISMONTANE** as an **UNFORTUITOUS LEVANTER** blew down. Encountering a **SCREE**, a **CHAMOIS**, and the **EFFLUVIUMS** of **TRAVERTINES**, we **HOVE** our rope, **HEEZED** ourselves up, and listened to a strange **DIAPASON**.

WORD	PART OF SPEECH ABBREVIATION	PRONUNCIATION	MEANING (IN SIMPLE LANGUAGE)
chivy			
fowling pieces			
cismontane			
unfortuitous			
levanter			
scree			
chamois			

ALL ABOUT WORDS: SPECTACULAR SENTENCES

WORD	PART OF SPEECH ABBREVIATION	PRONUNCIATION	MEANING (IN SIMPLE LANGUAGE)
effluviums			
travertines			
hove			
heezed			
diapason			

© Winebrenner, S. Rosson-Niess, S. & Stillman, C. (2024) Spectacular Sentences. San Diego: readersmagnet.com

Translation into Everyday Language

_____
_____
_____
_____
_____

Student's Name: _____

Classroom Name or Number: _____

SPECTACULAR SENTENCE #33

Emerging into an **IDYLLIC** clearing, most of the group members called others' attention to their own **CHARISMATIC TENDENCIES** except for one young **WHIPPERSNAPPER** who instantly started demonstrating his **CHARMANTIC PROCLIVITIES**, and a young **DAMSEL** who quickly started demonstrating some **INCONGRUOUS** behaviors which another member correctly identified as the **PSEUDOBULBAR AFFECT** and immediately **ABSQUATULATED**.

WORD	PART OF SPEECH ABBREVIATION	PRONUNCIATION	MEANING (IN SIMPLE LANGUAGE)
idyllic			
charismatic			
tendencies			
whippersnapper			
charmantic			
proclivities			
damsel			

ALL ABOUT WORDS: SPECTACULAR SENTENCES

WORD	PART OF SPEECH ABBREVIATION	PRONUNCIATION	MEANING (IN SIMPLE LANGUAGE)
incongruous			
pseudobulbar affect			
absquatulated			

© Winebrenner, S. Rosson-Niess, S. & Stillman, C. (2024) Spectacular Sentences. San Diego: readersmagnet.com

Translation into Everyday Language

_____
_____
_____
_____
_____

Student's Name: _____

Classroom Name or Number: _____

SPECTACULAR SENTENCE #34

Recent decades have witnessed some extraordinary accomplishments for astronauts working on **RECONNAISSANCE** activities carried out in space. For several decades, American men had **DOMINATED** missions into space; however, this changed as women earned more and more places on important missions. In fact, **PAUCILOQUENT** astronaut, Kristina Koch, became a new record holder for logging the most study results during extended space travel. Another **NOTEWORTHY** woman, Jessica U. Meir, is a NASA astronaut, marine biologist, and **PHYSIOLOGIST** who also served on several space missions. These two women **EVENTUALLY** found themselves serving together on the International Space Station (ISS), the habitable artificial satellite in low Earth orbit managed by 11+ countries from all over the world. Most remarkably, on October 18, 2019, Meir and Koch were the first US astronauts to participate in the **INAUGURAL** all-female spacewalk. Some applicants for this mission were denied access because they suffered from **HIPPOPOTOMONSTROSESQUIPPEDALIAOPHOBIA**.

WORD	PART OF SPEECH ABBREVIATION	PRONUNCIATION	MEANING (IN SIMPLE LANGUAGE)
reconnaissance			
dominated			
pauciloquent			
noteworthy			
physiologist			

ALL ABOUT WORDS: SPECTACULAR SENTENCES

WORD	PART OF SPEECH ABBREVIATION	PRONUNCIATION	MEANING (IN SIMPLE LANGUAGE)
eventually			
Inaugural			
hippopotomonstros- esquippedaliaophobia			

© Winebrenner, S. Rosson-Niess, S. & Stillman, C. (2024): Spectacular Sentences. San Diego: readersmagnet.com

Translation into Everyday Language

_____
_____
_____
_____
_____

Student's Name: _____

Classroom Name or Number: _____

If you wish, you may create your own SPECTACULAR SENTENCES from the words you find and record on the chart below, along with other sources you find. Please send the sentences you create to me at skwine76@gmail.com along with the below entry form. If selected, your spectacular sentence will be posted on my website! (www.susanwinebrenner.com).

CHALLENGE:

Your sentence and answer key must be included using the same type of table that has been used in the book. When creating your sentences, remember you can work alone or with 1 or 2 partners either at school or at home.

Whenever you create your own Spectacular Sentence that you are really proud of, **please post it on my website**. www.susanwinebrenner.com and click on "submit your super sentences here" (note that in order to post the sentence on our site for others to see, please ask one of your parents or a guardian to complete the entry form below and email it to me at skwine76@gmail.com. It would be especially helpful 'Spectacular Sentence' is in the subject line).

SPECTACULAR SENTENCES ENTRY FORM

I hereby grant permission for Susan Winebrenner and/or her affiliates to use the submitted Spectacular Sentence on her website and/or in other handouts they create and/or distribute.

_____   _____   _____
Name (Please Print)   Age   Current Grade in School

_____
City/Province/State/Country

_____
Signature of Parent or Guardian

To check to see if your spectacular sentence has been posted, please visit my website (www.susanwinebrenner.com) and check the section called SPECTACULAR SENTENCES.

SPECTACULAR SENTENCES ANSWER KEY

SPECTACULAR SENTENCE #1

An **ABSENT-MINDED** professor, whose summer **HABITAT** was a **DISMAL SHANTY**, was **FLABBERGASTED** to learn he had been **DULY BEQUEATHED** a **FASHIONABLE, PALATIAL MANSION** in a **LUXURIOUS GENTEEL** neighborhood.

WORD/PART OF SPEECH	PRONUNCIATION	MEANING
absentminded (adj)	ab' sent mīn dəd	preoccupied, forgetful
habitat (n)	ha'-bə-tat	place where one is commonly found living
dismal (adj)	diz' məl	dreary, cheerless
shanty (n)	shan' tē	crude building, usually temporary, shack
flabbergasted (v)	fla' bêr gas təd	shocked, overwhelmed
duly (adv)	doo' lē /(d(y)oo-lee	properly, as is right and fitting
bequeathed (v)	bi kwēthd'	left something in a will

WORD/PART OF SPEECH	PRONUNCIATION	MEANING
fashionable (adj)	fash'-uh nuh buhl	stylish
palatial (adj)	pə lā' shəl	like a palace
mansion (n)	man' shun	large home with many rooms
luxurious (adj)	lug shûr' ē əs	rich, very comfortable
genteel (adj)	jen tēl'	upper class, elegant

© Winebrenner, S. Rosson-Niess, S. & Stillman, C. (2024) Spectacular Sentences. San Diego: readersmagnet.com

TRANSLATION

A forgetful professor who lived in the summer in a cheerless, dreary shack, was shocked to learn he had been fittingly left, as a gift from someone who had died, a stylish, palace-like, huge home in a rich, elegant neighborhood.

SPECTACULAR SENTENCE #2

We live near a **GROTESQUE, HIDEOUS, DETERIORATED** old house, filled with **TORTUOUS, IMPENETRABLE** hallways which give me **EERIE, GHASTLY** feelings of **CLAUSTROPHOBIA** and **TREPIDATION**, especially when I hear the **FORMIDABLE CACOPHONY** of **BABBLING** voices when no one is there!

WORD/PART OF SPEECH	PRONUNCIATION	MEANING
grotesque (adj)	grō tesk'	distorted or absurd in appearance or shape
hideous (adj)	hid' ē əs	very ugly; revolting to look at
deteriorated (adj)	də tēr' ē ôr ā təd	run down; in need of repair
tortuous (adj)	tôr' choo əs	full of twists and turns
impenetrable (adj)	im pen' ə trə bəl	incapable of being penetrated
eerie (adj)	ē' rē	weird, strange
ghastly (adj)	gast' lē	horrible, frightful

WORD/PART OF SPEECH	PRONUNCIATION	MEANING
claustrophobia (n)	klos tro fo' bē ə	fear of closed-in places
trepidation (n)	trep ə dā' shun	fear or dread
formidable (adj)	fôr' mid ə bəl	awesome, dreadful
cacophony (n)	\kə-kä'-fə-nē	mixture of sounds that do not blend
babbling (adj)	ba'-b(ə-)liŋ	foolish, confused talking

© Winebrenner, S. Rosson-Niess, S. & Stillman, C. (2024) Spectacular Sentences. San Diego: readersmagnet.com

TRANSLATION

We live near an absurd-looking, ugly, run-down old house, filled with twisting halls that are impossible to get through, which give me weird, frightened feelings of the fear of being in a closed-in place, especially when I hear the dreadful, horrible-sounding noise of foolishly talking voices when no one is there.

SPECTACULAR SENTENCE #3

A ten-year-old boy was a dedicated **BIBLIOPHILE** and his twelve-year-old sister was an extraordinary **VERBIVORE**. They laughed so hard when they started tickling each other, they fell **CATTYWAMPUS** onto the floor where a **KERFUFFLE** began until their mom came to investigate. The children instantly fell into **IN CAHOOTS** and even increased their **EXTRAORDINARY VERBIGERATIONS** until their mom became even more **BUMFUZZLED** and **EXCORIATED** them more angrily than she intended.

WORD/PART OF SPEECH	PRONUNCIATION	MEANING
bibliophile (n)	bib′ lē ə fīl	a person who loves reading and books
verbivore (n)	ver′ bi vôr	a phrase person who loves of words and word play activities
cattywampus (adj)	cat e wam′ pus	items or people arranged in a way that seems to have no order or purpose
kerfuffle (n)	kur fuf′ əl	a disturbance or commotion; a fuss
(in) cahoots (n)	kə hoots	a secret agreement or cooperation for a particular purpose
extraordinary (adj)	ik-strawr-dn-er-ee	very unusual or remarkable
verbigeration(s) (n)	ver bij er ā′ shuns	the constant or obsessive repetition of meaningless words or phrases

WORD/PART OF SPEECH	PRONUNCIATION	MEANING
bumfuzzled (adj)	bum' fuz zeld	to confuse, perplex, or fluster one or more people
excoriated (v)	ex kôr ē āt ed	criticize or scold severely

© Winebrenner, S. Rosson-Niess, S. & Stillman, C. (2024) Spectacular Sentences. San Diego: readersmagnet.com

TRANSLATION

A ten-year-old boy was a dedicated book lover and his twelve-year-old sister was a huge fan of words and word play. They laughed so hard when they started tickling each other on the floor that it sounded like a huge commotion, causing their mom to come in and check out the fuss. The siblings continued laughing and repeating meaningless words and phrases which confused their mom even more, so she punished them more angrily than she had intended.

SPECTACULAR SENTENCE #4

My uncle, an **OBESE GOURMAND**, with his usual **APLOMB**, approached the table at my cousin's wedding **BANQUET** with such **ALACRITY** (**OBVIOUSLY** lacking **ADEQUATE FORESIGHT**) that he **INGESTED** what he thought was a **PALATABLE DELICACY**, which was actually the table's centerpiece. How **GAUCHE**!

WORD/PART OF SPEECH	PRONUNCIATION	MEANING
obese (adj)	ō bēs'	having a large, bulky, and heavy body
gourmand (n)	gôr mänd	person who appreciates fine food
aplomb (n)	ə plom'	complete confidence, assurance
banquet (n)	ban' kwet	a sumptuous feast; especially one attended by many people
alacrity (n)	ə lak' rə tē	cheerful readiness
obviously (adv)	ob' vē əs lē	clearly for all to see
adequate (adj)	ad' ə kwet	enough

WORD/PART OF SPEECH	PRONUNCIATION	MEANING
foresight (n)	fôr' sīt	ability to see ahead
ingested (v)	in jes' ted	swallowed; ate
palatable (adj)	pal' ə tə bəl	pleasant tasting
delicacy (n)	del' i kə sē	something unusual to eat
gauche (adj)	gōsh	lacking tact or the social graces; awkward

© Winebrenner, S. Rosson-Niess, S. & Stillman, C. (2024) Spectacular Sentences. San Diego: readersmagnet.com

TRANSLATION

My hugely overweight uncle, who appreciates fine food, with his usual complete confidence, approached the table with such cheerful readiness at the dinner in honor of my cousin's wedding, (clearly lacking enough ability to see what was coming) that he ate what he thought was a pleasant tasting, rare treat, which was actually the table's centerpiece. How awkward!

SPECTACULAR SENTENCE #5

The speaker showed his **ACUITY** on the subject while most of the students' faces bore a **STULTIFIED** expression, even though the speaker **PRESSED ON** with his **BRINKMANSHIP** that pushed the listeners to **UBIQUITOUSLY EXCORIATE** his techniques with their shared **PALPABLE** displeasure. This created an **ARDUOUS** continuation of the **RECALCITRANT** speaker's attempts to persuade the listeners that if they accepted his **TRANCENDENTAL** truths and blindly continued to accept his **OBFUSCATIONS** of accurate facts, they would eventually understand his message.

WORD/ PART OF SPEECH	PRONUNCIATION	MEANING
acuity (n)	a kyü' ə tē	sharpness of thoughts
stultified (v)	stul' ti fīd	to cause (someone) to become confused
pressed on (v)	prest on	continued
brinkmanship (n)	brink' man ship	pursue dangerous policy or practice to its boundary of danger
ubiquitously (adv)	you bik' wə tus lē	appears everywhere at the same time
excoriate (v)	ex kôr'ē āt	criticize forcefully
palpable (adj)	pal' pə bəl	able to be felt or experienced

WORD/PART OF SPEECH	PRONUNCIATION	MEANING
arduous (adj)	är'-jə-wəs	extremely difficult
recalcitrant (adj)	rē cal' si trant	uncooperative
transcendental (adj)	trans sen den' tal	philosophical belief system; going beyond ordinary beliefs
obfuscations (n)	ob fyü skā shuns	purposefully hide meaning from

© Winebrenner, S. Rosson-Niess, S. & Stillman, C. (2024) Spectacular Sentences. San Diego: readersmagnet.com

TRANSLATION

The speaker showed his sharpness of thought and accuracy of knowledge on the subject while most of the students' faces wore shocked expressions showing him that they were unable to understand. However, he continued ignoring those clues and forced the listeners to criticize his techniques.

SPECTACULAR SENTENCE #6

I faced the **CATACLYSMIC** event with what I hoped was an **ENIGMATIC** expression, hiding my usual **EGREGIOUS NATURE** and **NEFARIOUS** thoughts, proceeding with **TREPIDATION** and **DREAD**, to shout my **APPEALS** into the surrounding **QUAGMIRE**, hoping I would soon find some **CAMARADERIE**.

WORD/ PART OF SPEECH	PRONUNCIATION	MEANING
cataclysmic (adj)	kat ə kliz' mik	violent natural event
enigmatic (adj)	en ig ma' tik	mysterious
egregious (adj)	e grē' jus	shocking; even offensive in nature
nature (n)	nā' chûr	basic characteristics of something
nefarious (adj)	nə fār' ēus	highly offensive in character or conduct, extremely wicked
trepidation (n)	trep ə dā' shun	apprehension, uneasiness, worry
dread (n)	dred	great fear or apprehension

WORD/PART OF SPEECH	PRONUNCIATION	MEANING
appeals (n)	ə pēlz′	make a serious or urgent request
quagmire (n)	kwag′ mī(ə)r	hazardous; very difficult situation
camaraderie (n)	cäm rä′ de rē	a spirit of friendly good-fellowship

© Winebrenner, S. Rosson-Niess, S. & Stillman, C. (2024) Spectacular Sentences. San Diego: readersmagnet.com

TRANSLATION

I faced the violent event with a mysterious look in order to hide my usual shocked nature and offensive thoughts and proceeded cautiously to shout encouragingly at the difficult situation.

SPECTACULAR SENTENCE #7

My parents **AGONIZED** over whether to buy me a computer game with which I was **ENAMORED**, or a radio-controlled airplane, which I **LOATHED**. My **BERSERK** behavior let them know I was **DEVASTATED** by their choice, and they let me know they **RESENTED** my **OBJECTIONABLE, REBELLIOUS, TEMPERAMENTAL** reaction, and **ADMONISHED** me **EARNESTLY** to remember that everyone is **FALLIBLE**.

WORD/PART OF SPEECH	PRONUNCIATION	MEANING
agonized (v)	ag' ən īzd	suffered greatly over a decision; struggled
enamored (v)	en am' êrd	loved greatly; charmed with
loathed (v)	lōth'd	hated; detested
berserk (adj)	bêr sêrk'	crazy; out of control
devastated (v)	dev'ə stā ted	overwhelmed by disappointment
resented (v)	rē zen' ted	to feel bitter or indignant about
objectionable (adj)	əb jek' shən əbel	displeasure causing disapproval

WORD/PART OF SPEECH	PRONUNCIATION	MEANING
rebellious (adj)	ri-be'-lē-əs	opposing authority
temperamental (adj)	tem prə men' təl	tending to unpredictable behavior
admonished (v)	ad mon' ish'd	to criticize gently but earnestly
earnestly (adv)	êr' nest lē	in a serious and sincere manner
fallible (adj)	fal' ə bəl	capable of making a mistake

© Winebrenner, S. Rosson-Niess, S. & Stillman, C. (2024) Spectacular Sentences. San Diego: readersmagnet.com

TRANSLATION

My parents struggled over whether to buy me a computer game which I loved, or a radio-controlled airplane, which I hated. My crazy, out-of-control behavior let them know I was terribly disappointed with their choice; and they let me know they were displeased by my authority-opposing, unpredictable behavior of which they strongly disapproved, and earnestly advised me to remember that everyone can make a mistake.

SPECTACULAR SENTENCE #8

For a career in **AERONAUTICS, PREREQUISITES** include: a **DAUNTLESS, HEROIC** spirit, no **QUEASINESS** or **ACROPHOBIA**, the ability to **SKILLFULLY** operate **TECHNICAL APPARATUS**, and an **ENERGETIC DEVOTION** to the **GLORY** of American **DOMINANCE** in space.

WORD/PART OF SPEECH	PRONUNCIATION	MEANING
aeronautics (n)	ār ə nä' tiks	the science of designing or flying aircraft
prerequisites (n)	prē rek' wi zits	things required beforehand
dauntless (adj)	dawnt'-lis	bravely determined
heroic (adj)	her-oh-ik	having or showing qualities of courage and daring associated with heroes
queasiness (n)	kwē' zē nəs	uneasy, somewhat sick feeling
acrophobia (n)	ak rə fō' bē ə	fear of heights
skillfully (adv)	skil' fəl lē	having well-trained ability

WORD/PART OF SPEECH	PRONUNCIATION	MEANING
technical (adj)	tek′ ni kəl	having or showing specialized knowledge or skill in a particular field.
apparatus (n)	ap ə rat′ əs	equipment for a certain use or job
energetic (adj)	en êr jet′ ik	having a lot of energy
devotion (n)	dē vō′ shen	a strong feeling of love, respect, or admiration for someone or something
glory (n)	glôr′ ē	honor or praise
dominance (n)	dom′ ən ens	the state of being more powerful or important than other people or things

© Winebrenner, S. Rosson-Niess, S. & Stillman, C. (2024) Spectacular Sentences. San Diego: readersmagnet.com

TRANSLATION

For a career in flying aircraft, the things required beforehand include a bravely determined, courageous spirit, no uneasy feelings or fear of heights, the well-trained ability to operate equipment related to this science, and a strong attachment, accompanied by lots of energy, to the honor of the American ability to overcome all other countries in the space race.

SPECTACULAR SENTENCE #9

The **AUDACITY** of his actions, despite the **PAUCITY** of logical outcomes, led to the **AMBIVALENCE** of **PROPOUNDED** solutions which reflected the **PROSAIC** nature of his followers to discover a cure for the **MIASMA** of the swamp in question. The group created an **APHORISM** to describe this **MATTER AT HAND**: "Birds of a feather usually flock together", **ENCAPSULATING** the **PLETHORA** of poor ideas being explored by the group. As a reader, you are **AT LIBERTY** to create your own **APHORISM** describing this situation and send it to Susan at skwine76@gmail.com.

WORD/PART OF SPEECH	PRONUNCIATION	MEANING
audacity (n)	ä da' sə tē	boldness
paucity (n)	pau' sit ee	scarcity
ambivalence (n)	am biv' ə lence	the state of having mixed feelings or contradictory ideas about something or someone
propounded (v)	prə pound' ed	to put forth an idea
suggested (v)	səg jest' ed	put forward for consideration
prosaic (adj)	pro zā' ik	dull and unimaginative

WORD/PART OF SPEECH	PRONUNCIATION	MEANING
miasma (n)	mī'az mə	an oppressive or unpleasant atmosphere which surrounds or emanates from something
aphorism (n)	af' ôr izm	a short statement that expresses a truth or an opinion in a clever and amusing way
matter at hand (n)	mat' er at hand	topic or issue currently being discussed
encapsulating (v)	en'kap sə‚lāt ing	highlight the essential features of something
plethora (n)	pleth' êr ə	abundance
at liberty (adj)	at lib' êr tē	state of being free to do something

© Winebrenner, S. Rosson-Niess, S. & Stillman, C. (2024) Spectacular Sentences. San Diego: readersmagnet.com

TRANSLATION

The daring of his actions, in spite of the shortage of logical outcomes, led to the unclear direction to implement any of the unimaginative solutions brought forth by his followers to clear the horrible smell of the swamp in question. Instead, the group created a special saying to describe their situation. Feel free to create another saying to describe their abundance of poor solutions.

SPECTACULAR SENTENCE #10

Listening to the **LOQUACIOUS** gentleman's tale of his **AVARICIOUS** behavior in his **AUDACIOUS** pursuit of fame and wealth, I was struck by his **VORACIOUS** nature and his **DISINGENUOUS** ability to appear **VIVACIOUS** and even **OBSEQUIOUS** even though his actions were clearly **DUPLICITOUS** and **TREACHEROUS**.

WORD/PART OF SPEECH	PRONUNCIATION	MEANING
loquacious (adj)	lo kwā' shus	very talkative – uses many words
avaricious (adj)	av·a·ri'shəs	extreme greed for wealth or material gain
audacious (adj)	aw day' shəs	showing a willingness to take surprisingly bold risks
voracious (adj)	və rā' shəs	having an insatiable appetite for an activity or pursuit
disingenuous (adj)	dis en jen' yoo əs	not candid or sincere, typically by pretending that one knows less about something than one really does
vivacious (adj)	vī vā' shəs	highly spirited; center of attention
obsequious (adj)	əb sēk' wē əs	excessively eager to serve or please

WORD/PART OF SPEECH	PRONUNCIATION	MEANING
duplicitous (adj)	dü plis' ə təs	untrustworthy; says one thing and does another
treacherous (adj)	trech' êr əs	guilty of or involving betrayal

© Winebrenner, S. Rosson-Niess, S. & Stillman, C. (2024) Spectacular Sentences. San Diego: readersmagnet.com

TRANSLATION

Listening to the talkative gentleman's tale of his greedy behavior in his daring pursuit of fame and wealth, I was struck by his unstable nature in his misleading ability to appear highly spirited even though his actual behaviors were deceitful and dangerous.

SPECTACULAR SENTENCE #11

The **HEBETUDINOUS, LETHARGIC SCHOLAR** moved very slowly as though he was **DISTRACTED** from his learning, which he claimed to love for its own sake. He also claimed he was suffering from **CLINOMANIA** and his **THRASONICAL** behaviors caused his classmates to accuse him of trying to disturb their own learning with his **MALARKEY**. When his classmates discovered that he was also **ABIBLIOPHOBIC**, they wondered if he would ever be **SHREWD** enough to demonstrate his self-claimed **SAGACITY**.

WORD/PART OF SPEECH	PRONUNCIATION	MEANING
hebetudinous (adj)	heb ə tood' in us	moves very slowly; appears tired
lethargic (adj)	leth âr' jik	lacking energy
scholar (n)	sko' lîr	a person who has done advanced study in a special field
distracted (adj)	dis trak' ted	unable to concentrate or think clearly; preoccupied
clinomania (n)	klin ō mān' ē ə	loves staying in her bed all day
thrasonical (adj)	thra son' ə kəl	boastful; brags a lot
malarky (n)	mə lârk' ē	meaningless talk or writing; nonsense

WORD/PART OF SPEECH	PRONUNCIATION	MEANING
abibliophobic (adj)	ə bibliō fo' bik	fear of running out of things to read
shrewd (adj)	shrood	very clever; knows how to avoid being taken advantage of
sagacity (n)	sə gas' itē	deep knowledge/wisdom

© Winebrenner, S. Rosson-Niess, S. & Stillman, C. (2024) Spectacular Sentences. San Diego: readersmagnet.com

TRANSLATION

The slow-moving professional learner appeared to not be paying attention to his surroundings or to what was going on. He claimed he was suffering from a deep desire to stay in bed and had become very likely to brag about things he could do. He also expressed a fear of running out of things to read. Soon, other people concluded that although he was very clever, his deep knowledge was questioned by many people.

SPECTACULAR SENTENCE #12

The **BRAGGADOCIO** of the **POETASTER** is apparent as he writes his **CLOYING DITHYRAMBS** for **ACCOLADES** alone; while the **ORGULOUS IAMBOGRAPHER** has the **METTLE** and **PANACHE** to **EXCOGITATE** his **LAMPOONS** without **GASCONADE**.

WORD/PART OF SPEECH	PRONUNCIATION	MEANING
braggadocio (n)	brag ə dō' shē ō	empty boasting; arrogant pretension
poetaster (n)	pō' ət as têr	writer of poor poetry
cloying (adj)	kloy' ing	overly sweet or excessive
dithyrambs (n)	dith' ə ramz	a passionate or enthusiastic speech or piece of writing
accolades (n)	ak' ə lādz	recognition; bestowal of praise
orgulous (adj)	ôr' gyə ləs	proud
iambographer (n)	i am bä' gra fûr	one noted for writing iambic lampoons
mettle (n)	met' əl	courage

WORD/PART OF SPEECH	PRONUNCIATION	MEANING
panache (n)	pə näsh'	flair, elegant style, heroic flourish of manner
excogitate (v)	eks koj' i tāt	devise, contrive, think up; examine mentally in great detail
lampoons (n)	lam poonz'	a written or spoken attack using ridicule or sarcasm; a satire
gasconade (v)	gas' kən ād	excessive bragging

© Winebrenner, S. Rosson-Niess, S. & Stillman, C. (2024) Spectacular Sentences. San Diego: readersmagnet.com

TRANSLATION

The arrogant pretension of the bad writer of poetry is apparent as he writes his distastefully sentimental choral poems of praise just for recognition; while the writer of iambic satire has the courage and heroic style to devise his controversial satires without excessive bragging.

SPECTACULAR SENTENCE #13

In **CARTOMANCY**, **PRESTIDIGITATORS** who use **OBFUSCATION** and **PETTIFOGGERY** may live in **OBLOQUY** if a **CHARY, INDEFECTIBLE HARBINGER** of justice arises whose **ONUS** is to expose the **FEIGNED VERISIMILITUDE** of the practitioners as **CHICANERY**.

WORD/PART OF SPEECH	PRONUNCIATION	MEANING
cartomancy (n)	kär tə man' sē	art of fortune-telling using playing cards
prestidigitators (n)	pres tə dij' ə tā têrz	magicians
obfuscation (n)	ob fus kā' shun	act of bewildering, confusing
pettifoggery (n)	ped' e fog ə rē	the practice of engaging in chicanery
obloquy (n)	ob' lə kwē	disgrace; defaming utterances
chary (adj)	char' ē	careful; cautious
indefectible (adj)	in də fek' tə bəl	faultless; flawless; incorruptible
harbinger (n)	hâr' bin jêr	a sign of things to come

WORD/PART OF SPEECH	PRONUNCIATION	MEANING
onus (n)	ō' nus	burden; duty that involves considerable difficulty
feigned (adj)	fānd	to pretend; to make a false show of
verisimilitude (n)	vêr sə mil' ə tüd	something that appears to be truthful
chicanery (n)	shi kā' nə rē	trickery; deception

© Winebrenner, S. Rosson-Niess, S. & Stillman, C. (2024) Spectacular Sentences. San Diego: readersmagnet.com

TRANSLATION

In the art of fortune telling by using cards, magicians who use confusion and legal trickery may live in disgrace if a cautious, incorruptible herald of justice arises whose difficult duty is to expose the pretended appearance of truth of the practitioners as deception.

SPECTACULAR SENTENCE #14

The **CAITIFF USURPER, ACCOUTERED** for **MARAUDING** with his **JUNTA**, sought **IMPERIUM** for the **MOBOCRACY**, unaware of the **ANIMUS** of the **IMPUISSANT, LUMPEN DEMURRERS** ready to **IMMOLATE** themselves for the sake of their cause.

WORD/PART OF SPEECH	PRONUNCIATION	MEANING
caitiff (adj)	kā' tif	mean, evil, despicable, wretched
usurper (n)	yoo sûrp' êr	person who seizes power illegally
accoutered (v)	ə koo' têr'd	equipped, furnished
marauding (v)	mä rä' ding	roaming and looting
junta (n)	hoon' tə	a group of persons joined in political intrigue or conspiracy
imperium (n)	im pir' ē um	absolute power
mobocracy (n)	mo bo' krə sē	government by mob rule
animus (n)	an' i mus	hostility

WORD/PART OF SPEECH	PRONUNCIATION	MEANING
impuissant (adj)	im pyoo' sənt	powerless
lumpen (adj)	loom' pən	of inferior status in one's social class
demurrers (n)	də myûr' ērz	those who object
immolate (v)	im' mə lāt	sacrifice, usually in the interest of some cause

© Winebrenner, S. Rosson-Niess, S. & Stillman, C. (2024) Spectacular Sentences. San Diego: readersmagnet.com

TRANSLATION

The evil power seizer, equipped for roaming and looting with his military council, tried to get absolute power for his government that was ruled by a mob, unaware of the hostility of the powerless, who objected to his plan and were ready to sacrifice themselves for their cause.

SPECTACULAR SENTENCE #15

Because she had **DETECTED CHRONIC DEFICIENCIES** in our spelling recently, our teacher declared an **ULTIMATUM**: either we **RECTIFY** the **DECLINE** in our scores and **ACCRUE** several **CONSECUTIVE TRIUMPHS**, or we would have to **FORFEIT** our place as the **FOREMOST CONTRIBUTORS** to the school newspaper.

WORD/PART OF SPEECH	PRONUNCIATION	MEANING
detected (v)	dē tek' təd	discovered the existence of
chronic (adj)	krä'-nik	habitual or recurring over a long period
deficiencies (n)	dē fish' ən sēz	a lack or shortage of something needed or desirable
ultimatum (n)	ul ti mā' təm	final demand
rectify (v)	rek' ti fi	set something right
decline (v)	dē klīn'	to become less in amount, degree, quality, or strength
accrue (v)	ə kroo'	accumulate

WORD/PART OF SPEECH	PRONUNCIATION	MEANING
consecutive (adj)	kən-se'-kyə-tiv	uninterrupted; one after another
triumphs (n)	tri' umfs	victories
forfeit (v)	fôr' fit	lose the right to something
foremost (adj)	fôr' mōst	first in place or rank
contributors (n)	kən tri' byoo tərz	those who give something

© Winebrenner, S. Rosson-Niess, S. & Stillman, C. (2024) Spectacular Sentences. San Diego: readersmagnet.com

TRANSLATION

Because she had discovered recurring, unacceptable performances in our spelling recently, our teacher announced a final demand: either we improve our deteriorating scores and collect several uninterrupted victories, or we would have to give up our places as the primary donators of articles to the school newspaper.

SPECTACULAR SENTENCE #16

In the **FABULOUS, GRANDIOSE CHATEAU**, which has an **INCOMPARABLY IMPRESSIVE, PANORAMIC** view of the surrounding **TERRAIN**, the **GORGEOUS CHANDELIER** swayed **OMINOUSLY**, seconds before the **LETHAL** earthquake struck.

WORD/PART OF SPEECH	PRONUNCIATION	MEANING
fabulous (adj)	fab' yoo ləs	wonderful; incredible
grandiose (adj)	gran dē ōs' (gran' dē ōs)	impressive because of uncommon largeness, scope, effect, or grandeur
chateau (n)	sha tō'	a large castle or stately mansion
incomparably (adv)	in kom' pêr ə blē	in a manner that cannot be compared
impressive (adj)	im pres' iv	making a mark or impression
panoramic (adj)	pan er am' ik	unlimited view in all directions
terrain (n)	têr rān'	the feature of the land
gorgeous (adj)	gôr' jus	dazzlingly beautiful

WORD/PART OF SPEECH	PRONUNCIATION	MEANING
chandelier (n)	shan də lēr'	a decorative ceiling-mounted light fixture with branches for several lights
ominously (adv)	om' in us lē	suggesting that danger is coming
lethal (adj)	lē' thəl	causing death

© Winebrenner, S. Rosson-Niess, S. & Stillman, C. (2024) ASpectacular Sentences. San Diego: readersmagnet.com

TRANSLATION

In the incredibly wonderful and showy country house, which has an unlimited view of all the land around it that makes such a wonderful impression that it cannot be compared, the beautiful light fixture in the spacious room swayed, telling of coming danger, seconds before a killing earthquake struck.

SPECTACULAR SENTENCE #17

At the **FESTIVE**, **TESTIMONIAL REPAST** for our **FLAMBOYANT**, **DAPPER**, **DEBONAIR** principal, the guests ate **RAVENOUSLY** all the **DELECTABLE TIDBITS** which had been **PAINSTAKINGLY** prepared by our P.T.A.'s **ENTERPRISING** experts in the **CULINARY** arts.

WORD/PART OF SPEECH	PRONUNCIATION	MEANING
festive (adj)	fes' tiv	joyous, party-like
testimonial (n)	tes tə mō' nē əl	expression of appreciation
repast (n)	rē' past	a meal; also, the food served at a meal
flamboyant (adj)	flam boy' ənt	flashy, showy
dapper (adj)	dap' pêr	neat and trim in the way one dresses
debonair (adj)	deb ə nār'	gracefully charming
ravenously (adv)	rav' ən əs lē	very hungrily
delectable (adj)	də lek' tə bəl	enjoyable, delightful

WORD/PART OF SPEECH	PRONUNCIATION	MEANING
tidbits (n)	tid' bits	small pieces of food
painstakingly (adv)	pān' stā king lē	with great care
enterprising (adj)	en' têr pri zing	bold; loving to experiment; adventurous; original
culinary (adj)	koo' lin ār ē	related to the art of cooking

© Winebrenner, S. Rosson-Niess, S. & Stillman, C. (2024) Spectacular Sentences. San Diego: readersmagnet.com

TRANSLATION

At the party-like meal to show appreciation for our flashy, neat and charming principal, the guests ate very hungrily all the enjoyable choice bits of food which had been carefully prepared by our P.T.A.'s adventurous experts in the cooking arts.

SPECTACULAR SENTENCE #18

The **FETCHING** young woman with the **INTRIGUING** ability to **MESMERIZE** those around her was sometimes able to experience **UPWARD MOBILITY** which filled her heart with **EUPHORIA** and her bank account with **WINDFALLS**. These abilities appear to protect her from **BELLICOSE ENCOUNTERS** and **SPASMS** of internal fear about her future.

WORD/PART OF SPEECH	PRONUNCIATION	MEANING
fetching (adj)	fech' ing	beautiful
intriguing (adj)	in trēg' ing	fascinating
mesmerize (v)	mez' mûr īz	to attract and hold the attention of someone as if by magical or hypnotic power
upward mobility (n)	up' wêrd mō bil' it ē	the capacity for rising to a higher social or economic position
euphoria (n)	yoo fôr' ēə	complete satisfaction
windfalls (n)	wind' fälz	sudden unexpected gift
bellicose (adj)	bel' i kōs	looking for an argument

WORD/PART OF SPEECH	PRONUNCIATION	MEANING
encounters (n)	en cownt' êrz	meetings
spasms (n)	spa' zəmz	shaking; trembling/violent body reaction

© Winebrenner, S. Rosson-Niess, S. & Stillman, C. (2024) Spectacular Sentences. San Diego: readersmagnet.com

TRANSLATION

The beautiful and fascinating young woman with the ability to cast spells of appreciation over people was sometimes able to use that to move into a higher social group, which filled her heart with huge happiness and her bank account with sudden unexpected gifts. These abilities appear to also protect her from angry meetings and internal attacks of fear about her future.

SPECTACULAR SENTENCE #19

At the circus, a **FOOLHARDY, LOQUACIOUS HAWKER** stood in a **GARGANTUAN, GARISHLY** decorated wagon, trying to **BAMBOOZLE** and **BEFUDDLE** the people in the crowd, using **LINGO** to sell them a **CONCOCTION** which he **ASSERTED** would allow kids to **PROCURE** all A's in school if they **IMBIBED** one teaspoonful every morning.

WORD/PART OF SPEECH	PRONUNCIATION	MEANING
foolhardy (adj)	fül′ härd ē	foolishly adventurous
loquacious (adj)	lō kwā′ shəs	very talkative
hawker (n)	hä′ kêr	a person who travels about selling goods
gargantuan (adj)	gâr gan′ choo wən	huge, gigantic
garishly (adv)	gār′ ish lē	in a tastelessly or excessively showy manner
bamboozle (v)	bam boo′ zəl	to deceive by trickery
befuddle (v)	bē fud′ əl	to confuse or dull one's senses

WORD/PART OF SPEECH	PRONUNCIATION	MEANING
lingo (n)	lin' gō	language peculia to a certain group, jargon
concoction (n)	kən kok' shən	strange mixture
asserted (v)	ə sîr' təd	claimed, stated
procure (v)	prō kyûr'	obtain, get
imbibed (v)	im bīb' d	drank

© Winebrenner, S. Rosson-Niess, S. & Stillman, C. (2024) Spectacular Sentences. San Diego: readersmagnet.com

TRANSLATION

At the circus, a foolishly adventurous, talkative person who tries to sell things stood in a huge, tastelessly colorful wagon and tried to deceive with his tricks and confuse the senses of the people in the crowd, using peculiar words to sell them a strange mixture that he claimed would allow kids to earn all 'A's in school if they swallowed one teaspoonful every morning.

SPECTACULAR SENTENCE #20

The **MEWLING, INCONTINENT NEONATES** are **PURPORTED** to **REEK VENIAL, NOISOME FETORS** similar to those **EMANATING** from a **NOXIOUS, MEPHITIC CARAVANSERAI**.

WORD/PART OF SPEECH	PRONUNCIATION	MEANING
mewling (adj)	myool' ing	crying, whimpering
incontinent (adj)	in kon' tə nənt	unable to hold back one's bodily functions
neonates (n)	nē' ō nāts	newborn babies
purported (v)	pēr pôr' təd	claimed
reek (v)	rēk	give off a strong, offensive odor
venial (adj)	vē' nē l	excusable; forgivable
noisome (adj)	noy' səm	disgusting; offensive to the sense of smell
fetors (n)	fe' tərz	a strong, offensive odor; stench

WORD/PART OF SPEECH	PRONUNCIATION	MEANING
emanating (v)	em' ən āt ing	emitting, giving out from a source
noxious (adj)	nok' shəs	harmful to one's health
mephitic (adj)	mə fit' ik	offensive to the smell
caravanserai (n)	kar ə van' sə ri	an inn with a large courtyard in which camels rest overnight

© Winebrenner, S. Rosson-Niess, S. & Stillman, C. (2024) Spectacular Sentences. San Diego: readersmagnet.com

TRANSLATION

The crying babies with soiled diapers are claimed to give off excusable, disgusting odors similar to those surrounding an unhealthful, smelly inn where camels rest overnight.

SPECTACULAR SENTENCE #21

She appeared to be having trouble with several **IMPEDIMENTS** so that her sermon was full of **EQUIVOCATION** and thus was received with **MERETRICIOUS PERSIFLAGE** and **PROFLIGATE** disbelief even though she had a **PANACHE** about her. Unfortunately, several of the communicants viewed that attitude as **MENDACIOUS** and thus labeled her an **INVETERATE** liar.

WORD/PART OF SPEECH	PRONUNCIATION	MEANING
impediments (n)	im pe' də ments	an obstruction or hindrance
equivocation (n)	e quiv' ō kā shun	avoid letting others know your true opinion
meretricious (adj)	mār ə tri' shus	looks really good but has no substance
persiflage (n)	per si' fla'zh	light banter or conversation that suggests
profligate (adj)	prä' fli gāt	recklessly wasteful
panache (n)	pə nash'	appears to have much confidence
mendacious (adj)	men dā' shus	untruthful

WORD/PART OF SPEECH	PRONUNCIATION	MEANING
inveterate (adj)	in vet' êr āt	ingrained habit which is unlikely to change

© Winebrenner, S. Rosson-Niess, S. & Stillman, C. (2024) Spectacular Sentences. San Diego: readersmagnet.com

TRANSLATION

Because she was having trouble explaining her ideas in the speech, it appeared she was being untruthful, and her usual confidence was perceived as distrust by the audience.

SPECTACULAR SENTENCE #22

"Automan", the **MECHANICAL, AMBIDEXTROUS** robot, we own to do our **MENIAL** chores, caused a **FRENETIC HULLABALOO** when his **CIRCUITS** became **INOPERABLE,** and he ran **AMOK CAPRICIOUSLY** through our house, **DEFACING** everything in his path and leaving **IMPASSABLE PANDEMONIUM** everywhere.

WORD/PART OF SPEECH	PRONUNCIATION	MEANING
mechanical (adj)	mə kan' i kəl	operated automatically as by machine
ambidextrous (adj)	am bi dek' strəs	using both hands with equal ease
menial (adj)	mē' nē əl	a job that requires no special skill
frenetic (adj)	frə ne' tik	hurried; disordered; hectic
hullabaloo (n)	həl'ə bə loo	confused noise; uproar
circuits (n)	sîr' kuts	the path traveled by electricity
inoperable (adj)	in op' êr ə bəl	unable to be used

WORD/PART OF SPEECH	PRONUNCIATION	MEANING
amok (adv)	ə mək'	in a violently excited manner
capriciously (adv)	kə prish' əs lē	done or chosen seemingly at random or without method
defacing (v)	dē fā' sing	damaging the surface of something
impassable (adj)	im pas' ə bəl	impossible to move through
pandemonium (n)	pan də mō' nē əm	wild disorder

© Winebrenner, S. Rosson-Niess, S. & Stillman, C. (2024) Spectacular Sentences. San Diego: readersmagnet.com

TRANSLATION

"Automan," the automatic robot we own to do our simple chores, who could use his right and left hands with equal ease, caused a disordered uproar when his electrical pathways became impossible to operate, and he ran impulsively, in a violently excited manner, through our house, damaging the surfaces of everything in his path and leaving wild disorder everywhere through which it was impossible to move.

SPECTACULAR SENTENCE #23

The **MEED** for the **PROFLIGATE GORMANDIZER**, whose **IRREFRAGABLY CORPULENT PHYSIOGNOMY** betrayed his **UNABSTEMIOUS HYPOSTASIS**, and who refused to hold in **ABEYANCE** his **DRACONIC** appetite, was **DYSPEPSIA** and **KATZENJAMMER**.

WORD/PART OF SPEECH	PRONUNCIATION	MEANING
meed (n)	mēd	wage or reward; fitting return
profligate (adj)	pro' flə gāt	wildly extravagant or recklessly wasteful
gormandizer (n)	gôr' mən diz ér	lover of food who eats greedily
irrefragably (adv)	ir rə frag' ə blē	impossible to deny or dispute
corpulent (adj)	kôr' pyoo lənt	fat; obese; large body
physiognomy (n)	fız ē on' ə mē	outward features that show the inner qualities of mind or character
abeyance (n)	ə bā' əns	temporary suspension
draconic (adj)	drə kon' ik	dragon-like

WORD/PART OF SPEECH	PRONUNCIATION	MEANING
dyspepsia (n)	dis pep' sē ə	indigestion
katzenjammer (n)	kat' zen jam êr	a state of confusion or distress

© Winebrenner, S. Rosson-Niess, S. & Stillman, C. (2024) Spectacular Sentences. San Diego: readersmagnet.com

TRANSLATION

The fitting reward for the licentious lover of food, whose undeniably obese features betrayed his intemperate nature, and who refused to hold in temporary suspension his dragon-like appetite, was indigestion and a hangover.

SPECTACULAR SENTENCE #24

The visiting **PRELATE, INDAGATING MULTIFARIOUS** aspects of **TRADITIONALISM** by virtue of his **ACUMEN**, labored in the **CHANCEL** by the **SACRISTY** door, resisting the impulse to **SQUIB** a **POLEMICAL PAEAN** which would have been a **CONTRETEMPS** to his colleagues in the **CALEFACTORY**.

WORD/PART OF SPEECH	PRONUNCIATION	MEANING
prelate (n)	pre' lət	high-ranking church official
indagating (v)	in' də gā ting	investigating; researching
multifarious (adj)	mult ə fa' rē əs	having great diversity or variety
traditionalism (n)	trə di' shun əl ism	doctrine or practices of those who follow tradition; orientation toward old established values
acumen (n)	ə kyoo' mən	superior mental ability
chancel (n)	chan' sel	church area which contains altar, pulpit and lectern
sacristy (n)	sak' ris tē	room where sacred utensils and vestments are kept

WORD/PART OF SPEECH	PRONUNCIATION	MEANING
squib (n)	skwib	a short witty or satiric writing or speech
polemical (adj)	pə lem' i kəl	relating to or involving dispute or controversy
paean (n)	pē' ən	joyously exultant hymn
contretemps (n)	kon' trə tän	embarrassing or unexpected occurrence
calefactory (n)	kal ə fak' tə rē	heated parlor in a monastery

© Winebrenner, S. Rosson-Niess, S. & Stillman, C. (2024) Spectacular Sentences. San Diego: readersmagnet.com

TRANSLATION

The visiting high-ranking church official, researching the diverse aspects of the practice of established traditions easily because of his superior mental ability, worked in the pulpit area of the church by the door of the room where vestments are kept, resisting the impulse to write a witty satirical, caustic hymn which would have been an embarrassing occurrence to his colleagues in the heated parlor of the monastery.

SPECTACULAR SENTENCE #25

A **PLUVIOPHILE** finds **EUPHORIA** when the weather is **FORBIDDING** as it often **SUPPRESSES** an urge to **ENGAGE IN KLEPTOMANIA**. If one is in a place where **COLLOQUIALISMS** are the norms, they might seem to protect the **DISGRUNTLED** from **BELLICOSE** activity and **PAROXYSMS** of **OVERWHELMING** fear.

WORDS/PART OF SPEECH	PRONUNCIATION	MEANING
pluviophile (n)	ploo vēō' fīl	someone who loves the rain
euphoria (n)	yoo for' e ə	complete enjoyment
forbidding (adj)	for bid' ing	inspiring fear; intimidating
suppresses (v)	sup pres' sez	tries to make you stop
engage in (v)	en-geyj'	become involved
kleptomania (n)	klep tō main' ee ə	strong urge to take something that is not yours
colloquialism (n)	kə lō' kwee əl izm	word or expression from a certain geographic place

WORD/PART OF SPEECH	PRONUNCIATION	MEANING
disgruntled (adj)	dis grun' tld	very unhappy; dissatisfied
bellicose (adj)	bel-i-kohs	inclined or eager to fight; hostile; belligerent
paroxysms (n)	pair ox' zə smz	an attack of pain, laughter, rage, or other violent emotion
overwhelming (adj)	ō vêr welm' ing	overpowering in effect; too great or intense to be resisted

© Winebrenner, S. Rosson-Niess, S. & Stillman, C. (2024) Spectacular Sentences. San Diego: readersmagnet.com

TRANSLATION

A person who loves rain finds complete enjoyment when the weather is threatening, as it often overpowers an urge to take something that does not belong to him. If you are in a place where certain expressions and habits are normal, they might seem to protect the unsatisfied from angry activity and attacks of a huge amount of fear.

SPECTACULAR SENTENCE #26

The **PRODIGIOUS** and **PROLIFIC COGNOSCENTE** of modern music, **FESTINATING** to **TRANSCRIBE** the **SCHERZO** for winds and **TIMPANI**, **TRUNCATED** it to make a **SEGUE** between the **ITERATIVE, ANTIPHONAL**, and **ISACOUSTIC** sections of his new composition.

WORD/PART OF SPEECH	PRONUNCIATION	MEANING
prodigious (adj)	prə dij′ əs	extraordinary in size, amount, or degree
prolific (adj)	prō lif ′ ik	abundant and often rapid productivity
cognoscente (n)	käg-ˈnä-shen-tē	well-informed person
festinating (v)	fes′ tin ā ting	hastening, hurrying
transcribe (v)	trans skrīb′	rewrite; arrange a musical composition for different instruments, often with modification or embellishment
scherzo (n)	skär′ tzō	playful musical composition in quick triple time
timpani (n)	tim′ pən ē	a set of two or three kettle drums

WORD/PART OF SPEECH	PRONUNCIATION	MEANING
truncated (adj)	trun' kā təd	cut off a part; abbreviated
segue (n)	sā' gwā	transitional piece between musical numbers
iterative (adj)	it' êr â tiv	repetitious
antiphonal (adj)	an ti' fən əl	answering or alternating (voices or instruments)
isacoustic (adj)	i sə koo' stik	equally intense in sound

© Winebrenner, S. Rosson-Niess, S. & Stillman, C. (2024) Spectacular Sentences. San Diego: readersmagnet.com

TRANSLATION

The extraordinary person, well-informed and abundantly productive in the art of modern music, hurrying to arrange the fast, playful piece for winds and kettle drums, shortened it to make a transitional piece between the equally intense in sound sections of his new composition that repetitiously alternated instruments.

SPECTACULAR SENTENCE #27

The **TRUCULENT, OPPIDAN LICKSPITTLE SEQUESTERED** himself from the **BROUHAHA** caused by the **PUSILLANIMOUS MOUNTEBANK** and **MACHINATED** a **MACHIAVELLIAN PREVARICATION** to **METE** to himself some of the mountebank's **LUCRE.**

WORD/PART OF SPEECH	PRONUNCIATION	MEANING
truculent (adj)	truk' yə lənt	fierce, cruel, belligerent, pugnacious
oppidan (n)	äpədən	townsperson
lickspittle (n)	lik' spit əl	a flatterer; a toady
sequestered (v)	sə kwes' têr'd	secluded; separated
brouhaha (n)	broo hä' hä	excited clamor or confusion; hubbub
pusillanimous (adj)	pyoo sə lan' ə məs	cowardly
mountebank (n)	mown' tə bank	a charlatan or quack; one who sells pills or fake potions
machinated (v)	mak' ə nāt əd	contrived or devised; plotted

WORD/PART OF SPEECH	PRONUNCIATION	MEANING
Machiavellian (adj)	Mak ē ə vel' ē ən	resembling a political theory put forth by Machiavelli involving manipulation, duplicity; the belief that the end justifies the means
prevarication (n)	prē vār ə kā' shun	lie
mete (v)	mēt	distribute by careful measure, allot
lucre (n)	loo' kər	monetary collection; profit

© Winebrenner, S. Rosson-Niess, S. & Stillman, C. (2024) Spectacular Sentences. San Diego: readersmagnet.com

TRANSLATION

The cruel flatterer from the town separated himself from the confusion caused by the cowardly charlatan and devised a cleverly manipulative lie to allot to himself some of the mountebank's profit.

SPECTACULAR SENTENCE #28

Tigers can be **SAVAGE, FEROCIOUS, COMBATIVE** animals. Tiger trainers should not be too **ARROGANT** or **CONCEITED**, or they might have to **GRAPPLE DEFENSIVELY** with a **VORACIOUS, BELLIGERENT CARNIVORE** that would **APPARENTLY** be **VICTORIOUS**.

WORD/PART OF SPEECH	PRONUNCIATION	MEANING
savage (adj)	sav' əj	wild, fierce
ferocious (adj)	fə rō' shus	fierce, savage
combative (adj)	kəm bat' iv	eager to fight
arrogant (adj)	ār' ə gənt	overconfident, having a feeling of superiority
conceited (adj)	kən sē' təd	having too high an opinion of oneself
grapple (v)	gra'pəl	seize or hold onto
defensively (adv)	də fen' siv lē	in a way that is meant to protect oneself against attack or criticism
voracious (adj)	vō rā' shus	extremely hungry; ravenous

WORD/PART OF SPEECH	PRONUNCIATION	MEANING
belligerent (adj)	bə lij' êr ənt	eager to fight
carnivore (n)	kâr' nə vôr	animal that eats other animals or humans
apparently (adv)	ə par' ənt lē	obviously; plainly; likely
victorious (adj)	vik tôr' ē əs	triumphant; winning

© Winebrenner, S. Rosson-Niess, S. & Stillman, C. (2024) Spectacular Sentences. San Diego: readersmagnet.com

TRANSLATION

Tigers can be wild, fierce animals that are eager to fight. Tiger trainers should not be too over-confident or think too highly of their ability or they might have to try to grab, in order to defend themselves, an extremely hungry, ready-to-fight, flesh-eater which would likely be the winner.

SPECTACULAR SENTENCE #29

The **SENESCENT MYSTAGOGUE, DIVAGATING** from **LUCULENT** interpretations and **SPOUTING ABSTRUSE CANT, MESMERIZED** the **PURBLIND NEOPHYTES** who were **AGOG** at his supposed **SAGACITY**.

WORD/PART OF SPEECH	PRONUNCIATION	MEANING
senescent (adj)	sə nes' ənt	aging
mystagogue (n)	mis' tə gog	interpreter of mysteries; teacher of mystical doctrines
divagating (v)	di və gā' ting	wandering; straying
luculent (adj)	lü' kyoo lənt	clear; convincing
spouting (v)	spow' ting	pouring out words
abstruse (adj)	ab strüs'	hard to understand; hidden (idea)
cant (n)	kant	insincere talk; use of pious phraseology
mesmerized (v)	mez' mêr iz'd	caused to be spellbound; fascinated

WORD/PART OF SPEECH	PRONUNCIATION	MEANING
purblind (adj)	pêr' blind	newly blind; comprehending imperfectly
neophytes (n)	nē' ō fītz	new convert
agog (adj)	ə gog'	eager; curious; excited; intensely interested
sagacity (n)	sə gas' ə tē	quality of being discerning; keenly perceptive

© Winebrenner, S. Rosson-Niess, S. & Stillman, C. (2024) Spectacular Sentences. San Diego: readersmagnet.com

TRANSLATION

The aging teacher of mystical doctrines, straying from clear interpretations and pouring out hard-to-understand, pious phraseology, held spellbound the new converts who comprehended imperfectly and were excited about his supposed keen perception.

SPECTACULAR SENTENCE #30

The **UNCONSCIONABLE MALFEASANTS** of the **KAKISTOCRACY** had a **PROCLIVITY** to **PRATE INDEFATIGABLY** in their own **ARGOT** and would **JUGULATE** any **TIMOROUS PROSELYTE** who held an opinion **MINACIOUS** or **PARLOUS** to them.

WORD/PART OF SPEECH	PRONUNCIATION	MEANING
unconscionable (adj)	un kon' shun ə bəl	not fair or just; outrageous
malfeasants (n)	mal fēz' ənts	officials guilty of wrongdoing, especially in connection with the office
kakistocracy (n)	kak i stok' rə sē	government by the worst people in the country
proclivity (n)	prō kliv' i tē	natural tendency
prate (v)	prāt	to talk excessively; babble
indefatigably (adv)	in də fat' ə gə bəly	continuing unremittingly, untiringly
argot (n)	är gō	special vocabulary that belongs to a particular group or profession; jargon
jugulate (v)	joo' gyu lāt	cut the throat of

WORD/PART OF SPEECH	PRONUNCIATION	MEANING
timorous (adj)	tim' êr əs	fearful; timid
proselyte (n)	pros' ə lit	a convert to a new belief
minacious (adj)	mi nā' shus	menacing; threatening
parlous (adj)	pâr' ləs	perilous; dangerous

© Winebrenner, S. Rosson-Niess, S. & Stillman, C. (2024) Spectacular Sentences. San Diego: readersmagnet.com

TRANSLATION

The unjust public officers (guilty of wrongdoing) in the government run by the worst people in the country had a natural tendency to babble untiringly in their own jargon and would cut the throat of any timid convert who held an opinion threatening or dangerous to them.

SPECTACULAR SENTENCE #31

In my **SOLITUDE**, I find **SERENDIPITY** when other **AFFICIONADOS**, who are **UBIQUITOUS** in my **QUAINT**, **IDYLLIC** neighborhood, over-populated by **XENOPHOBES** with a **PARLANCE** all their own, sometimes become actually **OBSTREPEROUS** when they discover the **CONUNDRUMS**, they are discussing are the **EPITOME** of senselessness.

WORD/PART OF SPEECH	PRONUNCIATION	MEANING
solitude (n)	säl' ə tüd	a time when one is totally alone
serendipity (n)	sār en dip' i dē	the occurrence of events by chance in a happy or beneficial way
afficionados (n)	ə fish' ē un nä' dōs	a person who likes, knows about, and appreciates a particular interest or activity
ubiquitous (adj)	yü bik' kwi tus	everywhere at once
quaint (adj)	kwānt	attractively unusual or old-fashioned
idyllic (adj)	ī di' lik	extremely happy, peaceful, or picturesque
xenophobes (n)	zēn' ō fōbs	a person who has strong feelings of suspicion or hatred for people who are not from their own country or region.

WORD/PART OF SPEECH	PRONUNCIATION	MEANING
parlance (n)	par' lens	the unique ways in which people from certain locations or in certain professions speak
obstreperous (adj)	əb strep'er us	noisy or difficult; intrusive
conundrums (n)	kə nən' drəmz	problem that seems to defy easy solutions
epitome (n)	e pit' ə me	the height of... (experiences such as rudeness or happiness)

© Winebrenner, S. Rosson-Niess, S. & Stillman, C. (2024) Spectacular Sentences. San Diego: readersmagnet.com

TRANSLATION

When I am alone, I find fans, who are everywhere in my unusual, perfect neighborhood which has too many people who are very suspicious of people who look different with a special language only a few of them understand, who sometimes become irritatingly uncooperative, when they discover the senseless topics, they are discussing are the height of not making any sense.

SPECTACULAR SENTENCE #32

On a **CHIVY** with our **FOWLING PIECES**, we approached the **CISMONTANE** as an **UNFORTUITOUS LEVANTER** blew down. Encountering a **SCREE**, a **CHAMOIS**, and the **EFFLUVIUMS** of **TRAVERTINES**, we **HOVE** our rope, **HEEZED** ourselves up, and listened to a strange **DIAPASON**.

WORD/PART OF SPEECH	PRONUNCIATION	MEANING
chivy (n)	shiv' ē	chase or hunt
fowling pieces (n)	fow' ling pēs' əz	light gun for shooting birds or small animals
cismontane (adj)	sis' mon' tān	nearer side of a mountain
unfortuitous (adj)	un fôr tü' ə tus	unlucky
levanter (n)	lə van' têr	strong, easterly Mediterranean wind
scree (n)	skrē	loose rock on a mountain slope
chamois (n)	sham' ē or sham' wä	mountain antelope

WORD/PART OF SPEECH	PRONUNCIATION	MEANING
effluviums (n)	e floo′ vē ums	slight vapors; emanation; exhaust
travertines (n)	trav′ êr tenz	mineral deposits around hot springs
hove (v)	hōv	threw; hurled; lifted
heeze(d) (v)	hēz′d	hoisted; raised; pulled up
diapason (n)	di ə pā′ zən	burst of (harmonious) sound

© Winebrenner, S. Rosson-Niess, S. & Stillman, C. (2024) Spectacular Sentences. San Diego: readersmagnet.com

TRANSLATION

On a bird hunting chase with light guns, we approached the near side of the mountain as an unlucky strong easterly Mediterranean wind blew down. Encountering a slope of loose rock, a mountain antelope, and the slight vapors of hot springs mineral deposits, we hurled our rope, hoisted ourselves up, and listened to a burst of harmonious sound.

SPECTACULAR SENTENCE #33

Emerging into an **IDYLLIC** clearing, most of the group members called others' attention to their own **CHARISMATIC TENDENCIES** except for one young **WHIPPERSNAPPER** who instantly started demonstrating his **CHARMANTIC PROCLIVITIES**, and a young **DAMSEL** who quickly started demonstrating some **INCONGRUOUS** behaviors which another member correctly identified as the **PSEUDOBULBAR AFFECT** and immediately **ABSQUATULATED**!

WORD/PART OF SPEECH	PRONUNCIATION	MEANING
idyllic (adj)	ī di' lik	absolutely perfect
charismatic (adj)	ker' əz ma' tik	attracts everyone
tendencies (n)	ten' den sēs	natural impulses
whippersnapper (n)	(h)wi' pər sna pər	a young and inexperienced person considered to be overconfident
charmantic (adj)	shar man' tik	charming, agreeable, nice
proclivities (n)	prō kliv' ə tēz	repetitive habits
damsel (n)	dam' zel	young lady

WORD/PART OF SPEECH	PRONUNCIATION	MEANING
incongruous (adj)	in kän grə' wəs	inconsistent; absurd; illogical; inappropriate
pseudobulbar affect (n)	pseu' dō bəl bər ə fekt'	sudden, frequent, uncontrollable outbursts of crying or laughing
absquatulated (v)	abz kwä' chə lāt ed	to leave without saying goodbye

© Winebrenner, S., Rosson-Niess, S., & Stillman, C. (2022): Spectacular Sentences. San Diego: Readers Magnet.com

TRANSLATION

Emerging into a perfectly beautiful clearing, most of the group members called other's attention to their own highly attractive appearance, except for one young overconfident male who instantly started demonstrating his charmingly romantic tendencies, and a young lady, who quickly started demonstrating some absurd behaviors which another member correctly identified as switching from laughing to crying without warning and immediately left the without saying goodbye!

SPECTACULAR SENTENCE #34

Recent decades have witnessed some extraordinary accomplishments for astronauts working on **RECONNAISSANCE** activities carried out in space. For several decades, American men had **DOMINATED** missions into space; however, this changed as women earned more and more places on important missions. In fact, **PAUCILOQUENT** astronaut, Kristina Koch, became a new record holder for logging the most study results during extended space travel. Another **NOTEWORTHY** woman, Jessica U. Meir, is a NASA astronaut, marine biologist, and **PHYSIOLOGIST** who also served on several space missions. These two women **EVENTUALLY** found themselves serving together on the International Space Station (ISS), the habitable artificial satellite in low Earth orbit managed by 11+ countries from all over the world. Most remarkably, on October 18, 2019, Meir and Koch were the first US astronauts to participate in the **INAUGURAL** all-female spacewalk. Some applicants for this mission were denied access because they suffered from **HIPPOPOTOMONSTROSESQUIPPEDALIAOPHOBIA**.

WORD/PART OF SPEECH	PRONUNCIATION	MEANING
reconnaissance (n)	rē ko' nə sens	checking out conditions before starting a project
dominated (v)	do' min ā ted	to exert the supreme determining or guiding influence on
pauciloquent (adj)	pä si' lō kwənt	uttering few words; brief in speech
noteworthy (adj)	nōt' wêr thē	worthy of or attracting attention especially because of some special excellence
physiologist (n)	fi zē äl' ə jist	biological scientist who studies how plants and animals function under both normal and abnormal conditions.

WORD/PART OF SPEECH	PRONUNCIATION	MEANING
eventually (adv)	ē ven' choo ə lē	at some time in the future
inaugural (adj)	i nä' gûr əl	marking a beginning; first in a projected series
hippopotomonstroses quippedaliophobia (n)	ˌhi-pə-ˌpä-tə-män-ˌstrō-səs-ˌkwip-də-'lī-ə-ˌfō-bē-ə	an exaggerated fear of long words

© Winebrenner, S. Rosson-Niess, S. & Stillman, C. (2024) Spectacular Sentences. San Diego: readersmagnet.com

TRANSLATION

Recent decades have witnessed some extraordinary accomplishments for astronauts working on activities that help scientists figure out how to make missions work better. For several decades, American men had dominated missions into space. That changed as women earned places in important missions. For example, in early 2020 Kristina Koch became the new record holder for the female who has logged the most scientific studies on extended space travel. Jessica U. Meir is a NASA astronaut, marine biologist, and physiologist. These two women worked together on the International Space Station (ISS), where several members from different countries came together to work on tasks collaboratively. Koch and Meir were among the astronauts to complete an all-female mission to the ISS.

SPECTACULAR SENTENCES RECORD KEEPING FORMS

SENTENCE COMPLETION LOG

Keep track of which sentences you complete in this log.

SENTENCE #	DATE COMPLETED	COMMENTS

SENTENCE #	DATE COMPLETED	COMMENTS

ALL ABOUT WORDS: SPECTACULAR SENTENCES

SENTENCE #	DATE COMPLETED	COMMENTS

YOUR OWN WORD LIST

WORD	PART OF SPEECH	MEANING

YOUR OWN WORD LIST

WORD	PART OF SPEECH	MEANING

YOUR OWN WORD LIST

WORD	PART OF SPEECH	MEANING

www.ingramcontent.com/pod-product-compliance
Ingram Content Group UK Ltd.
Pitfield, Milton Keynes, MK11 3LW, UK
UKHW050414240426
12048UKWH00020B/1503